PRINCIPLES OF LIFE INSURANCE

A Textbook for Post Graduate Diploma in Insurance

Dr. Shrikrishna Laxman Karve
B.Com. (Stat.), LL.B., M.A., Ph.D., FIII

Himalaya Publishing House
ISO 9001:2008 CERTIFIED

FIRST EDITION : 2003
SECOND EDITION : 2009
REPRINT : 2013
REPRINT : 2017

Published by : Mrs. Meena Pandey for **Himalaya Publishing House Pvt. Ltd.**, "Ramdoot", Dr. Bhalerao Marg, Girgaon, **Mumbai - 400 004.** Phone: 022-23860170/23863863, Fax: 022-23877178 **E-mail: himpub@vsnl.com; Website: www.himpub.com**

Branch Offices :

New Delhi : "Pooja Apartments", 4-B, Murari Lal Street, Ansari Road, Darya Ganj, New Delhi - 110 002. Phone: 011-23270392, 23278631; Fax: 011-23256286

Nagpur : Kundanlal Chandak Industrial Estate, Ghat Road, Nagpur - 440 018. Phone: 0712-2738731, 3296733; Telefax: 0712-2721216

Bengaluru : Plot No. 91-33, 2nd Main Road Seshadripuram, Behind Nataraja Theatre, Bengaluru-560020. Phone: 08041138821, 9379847017, 9379847005

Hyderabad : No. 3-4-184, Lingampally, Besides Raghavendra Swamy Matham, Kachiguda, Hyderabad - 500 027. Phone: 040-27560041, 27550139

Chennai : New No. 48/2, Old No. 28/2, Ground Floor, Sarangapani Street, T. Nagar, Chennai - 600 012. Mobile: 09380460419

Pune : First Floor, "Laksha" Apartment, No. 527, Mehunpura, Shaniwarpeth (Near Prabhat Theatre), Pune - 411 030. Phone: 020-24496323/24496333; Mobile: 09370579333

Lucknow : House No. 731, Shekhupura Colony, Near B.D. Convent School, Aliganj, Lucknow - 226 022. Phone: 0522-4012353; Mobile: 09307501549

Ahmedabad : 114, "SHAIL", 1st Floor, Opp. Madhu Sudan House, C.G. Road, Navrang Pura, Ahmedabad - 380 009. Phone: 079-26560126; Mobile: 09377088847

Ernakulam : 39/104 A, Lakshmi Apartment, Karikkamuri Cross Rd., Ernakulam, Cochin - 622011, Kerala. Phone: 0484-2378012, 2378016; Mobile: 09387122121

Bhubaneswar : 5 Station Square, Bhubaneswar - 751 001 (Odisha). Phone: 0674-2532129, Mobile: 09338746007

Kolkata : 108/4, Beliaghata Main Road, Near ID Hospital, Opp. SBI Bank, Kolkata - 700 010, Phone: 033-32449649, Mobile: 7439040301

Printed at : Infinity Imaging System, New Delhi. On behalf of HPH

PREFACE

This is a Textbook for Post-Graduate Diploma in Insurance. Insurance business is now thrown open to private enterprise. We have as of now a dozen private Insurers each in Life Insurance and General Insurance Sectors. With IRDA's active regulation, Insurance sector is poised for well-sustained growth in future. Public interest in Insurance is growing. While the prospective agents study the Text Book prepared by Insurance Institute of India, paucity of such book for general public was keenly felt. Insurance is now receiving serious attention by colleges and universities also. This text book prepared as a part of the Study course for post graduate Diploma in Insurance would be found useful also to a layman who wants to know about the basics of Life Insurance. It will satisfy the needs of student population in general as well.

S.L. Karve

CONTENTS

1 Life Insurance — Principles

Objectives

To provide an understanding of the elementary principles of life insurance and their relevance.

Lesson Objectives

To enable the students to understand:

(1) The need for security, against economic difficulties, risk and uncertainty.

(2) The nature and uses of Life Insurance.

INTRODUCTION

1. Search for Security

Human beings have been in search of security right from nomadic days. The history of mankind is a history of the search for security. Man had to face dangers and risks which threatened his very existence. As an individual he would have found it difficult to combat these external dangers. He therefore started living in a group, thereby ensuring group security and cover against possible external dangers. The greatest risk was, of course, that of death, from wild animals, snakes, crocodiles and other crawling creatures and also from natural calamities, such as floods, fires and earthquakes.

As human society developed, commerce and business started flourishing and idea of insurance was promoted in due course. *Insurance is the group effort to reduce the sufferings of an individual as a result of some inevitable calamities.* Death, disability, sickness – are important examples. Loss of property due to external forces also worried the individual human being. The obvious solution was *Insurance*.

> For the provision of protection to life and property, human beings facing the same or similar risks came together and shared in advance the probable future loss that might take place due to specified reasons under specified circumstances, during a specified period. This idea of collective protection was practiced even in ancient society.

In India, the idea of insurance finds expression in the famous word Yogakshema (meaning protecting what has come and using the same for the welfare of the concerned people). References to Yogakshema are found in the Rigveda as well as in various Smritis of different periods.

Kautilya, in his Arthashastra, lays down that the people agree to pay taxes so that they are maintained by those taxes. The king himself should maintain children, aged persons and persons in distress, women without children and the children of helpless persons. It was the duty of the elders to maintain the property of a minor till he attained majority. The system of the joint family, which was a natural outcome of Janpad society, practised this concept of sharing individual losses – ensuring co-operation, moral restraint, tolerance and savings. It ensured the division of labour reducing the cost of production, equitable distribution of joint family profits and overall social and economic security.

In the wake of industrialisation, consequent urbanisation and breakup of the joint family system, an alternative was sought and that was provided by Insurance. *This search for security is a never-ending process.* With the advent of civilization, the nature of security needed by various human groups is also changing.

Man needs food, shelter and clothing for his survival. For the satisfaction of these needs, he requires money; which comes from his earnings. Earnings are a result of the capacity to earn, which may be extinguished by death or threatened by old age or disability. These may result in the stoppage of income or the reduction in income which is necessary for him and his family's sustenance.

If the breadwinner lives a normal span of life, the financial arrangements which he would have made for himself and his family members would have been fulfilled. However if he happens to die early (premature death), his family would be deprived of the income, which the deceased would have brought-in, had he not died.

The alternative arrangements for such an eventuality can be made with the help of life insurance.

> The greatest risk to which human life is exposed is that of death. Though death is certain, the time when it will strike is uncertain. This uncertainty gives rise to insurance. Insurance cannot avoid this uncertainty, what Insurance seeks to ensure is the replacement or reimbursement of financial/economic consequences if such an event takes place. Insurance cannot postpone the event. The insured event cannot be brought about earlier.

In that event, there would not be any insurance. For example, a person committing suicide after taking insurance cannot expect the insurance company to pay the policy amount (sum assured) after such an event. In other words, the insured person should not cause the insured event to take place.

Since insurance seeks to deal with the financial consequences of the risk, apart from death, *living too long is also a risk,* because everyday we need money for our sustenance. Apart from natural death and a long life, human beings are exposed to the following risks.

Disability — Natural: This is normally not covered by a life insurance policy. Accidental Disability can however be covered by a life insurance policy as an additional benefit (rider benefit) by paying an additional premium (rider premium) usually at the rate of Re.1/- per thousand sum assured per year, over and above the usual premium. Some policies include this amount in the basic premium itself.

Double Accident benefit consists of payment of double the sum assured in the event of a person's death due to accident. Sickness policies are covered by a general insurance policy. However, a life insurance policy may cover some specified sicknesses/illnesses, either by charging an extra premium (rider premium) or by giving it as an additional benefit, by enhancing the basic premium itself.

2. Individual Life Insurance

Started in 18th century in England. The first-ever Mortality Table was prepared by Mr. Carlisle on the basis of death-statistics of a county church. Soon Mortality Tables for all-England were prepared. The basic policy was issued in the form of One Years' Term Assurance (OYTA). However the scheme did not work for want of a sufficient number of normal lives to make the scheme viable. The insurance companies tried single premium policies but did not find it to be a workable scheme. *Finally a solution was found in the form of level premium/uniform premium — which practice continues even today.*

As age increases, the probability of dying in the next year increases. The rate of dying for a particular age is called Mortality. *The higher the age, the higher the mortality and since premium that is charged must be adequate for the mortality (risk) involved, the higher the age, the higher the premium.* But under a level premium plan, a company collects a higher premium than necessary, to cover the risk for that premium. This applies to most of the individual life insurance plans.

Individual life insurance policies were issued as Term Assurances. The insured person pays a small premium to get death risk cover for a period of one year on his life. If the insured person does not die within the insured period, the premium paid by him will not be refunded because even though he has not died, some other persons from his group would have died, for whom the company is required to pay the death claim. When OYTA is extended to a longer period, the insured person pays a predetermined premium for the specified period. If, the death takes place during this period, the company pays the agreed sum assured, as stated in the policy document. This is real Term Assurance. *If this is renewed from year to year, it becomes One Years' Renewable Term Assurance (OYRTA). In actual practice Level Premium has replaced OYRTA, which is however practised in Group Insurance Business, where the premium changes every year.*

Individual Term Assurance Plans were not popular in India, though in the western world these are quite common and popular. Of late, however, with the entry of private insurance companies into the field, term insurances are being sold by most companies, including LIC of India.

Term Assurance, as its name suggests, satisfies a particular need namely financial provision in case of premature death of the bread-winner. Individual life insurance seeks to satisfy a particular need of the individual. This need may be immediate, such as providing collateral security for housing or any other loan, or it may be a future need, such as providing a tidy sum on attainment of a particular age. The first need would be satisfied by taking out a Term Assurance Policy, while the second need would be satisfied by taking out an endowment type of policy. If the amount is needed, not after many years but in the near future say after 5 or 10 years, a money-back-type of policy can serve the purpose. For financial protection of a property in case of owner's premature death, the Term Assurance should serve the purpose. For those who look on Insurance as investment, Life Insurance does offer investment-centred or investment-oriented plans such as Bima Plus or Bima Nivesh Policies of LIC. Business partners can go in for Joint Life Insurance on their lives. Under this plan, the sum assured becomes payable on the first death or on completion of the term. Life Assurance policies are freely assignable under Section 38 of Insurance Act, 1938. The policyholder can assign his rights, title and interest in the policy to a Third Party either for valuable consideration or to a near-relative out of natural love and affection. Assignment in favour of a wife can be secured by taking out a life insurance policy in terms of the Married Women's Property Act, 1874. In such an event an immediate trust is created in favour of the wife as a trustee. This policy is essentially taken for the benefit of children, who are named as beneficiaries. Some persons, who are in the upper or marginal income tax bracket, take a life insurance policy to claim rebate against Income Tax in terms of relevant sections of Income Tax Act 1961 — *viz.* Sec. 88 & 80CCC.

3. The needs for life insurance may vary from person to person and for the same person be different at different life stages. Moreover, what is a luxury today or not a need today can became a need in future. Conversely what is a need today may not be so in future.

A.H. Maslow, a British psychologist, divided human needs on a 5-level basis. The basic foremost need is common to all human beings. Physiological needs — food, shelter and clothing are the prime needs which every human being has to satisfy. In fact a major part of a person's earnings is utilised in satisfying these needs. The peculiarity of these needs is that a person is not satisfied after satisfaction of one need or one-level of need. He likes to move on to the next higher need. The need to seek protection or safety from extraneous factors follow. In Maslow's terms this is a lower order need. These follow higher order needs.

MASLOW'S DIAGRAM OF NEED-BASED HIERARCHY

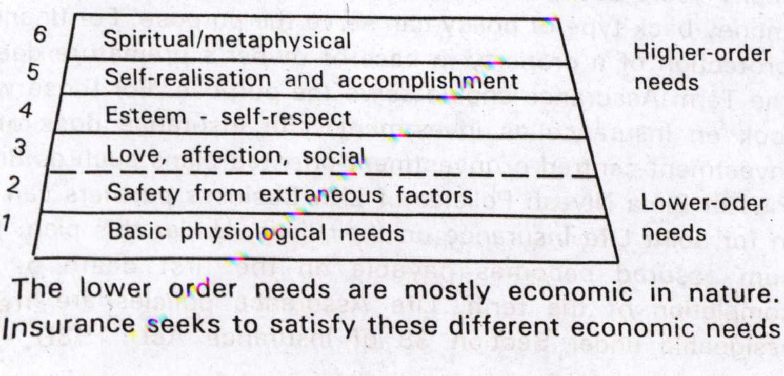

The lower order needs are mostly economic in nature. *Life* Insurance seeks to satisfy these different economic needs of different persons at different times. Hence, it is said that Life Insurance has no substitute.

Classification of Needs

(1) *Clean-up Fund:* This is required for meeting hospital/medical bills during terminal sickness, outstanding housing loans, bank loans etc.

(2) Income during dependency period, i.e., the period immediately following the death of the bread-winner.

(3) Self-supporting fund for the widow/widower.

(4) To tide over economic dislocation caused by the death of the housewife.

(5) Repayment of housing loan (and interest thereon) raised by the deceased bread-winner, so that the ownership and possession of the house are not disturbed and the purpose for which housing loan was raised. i.e., of providing shelter and roof to near and dear ones is not defeated.

(6) Raising Educational/Marriage Fund for children.

(7) Insurance needs of business organisation.

(8) Keyman insurance — to take care of situation arising out of death of Keyman.

(9) Generation of sufficient post retirement income to help the person to maintain the earlier life-style.

> Life Insurance thus satisfies two basic needs
> (a) economic protection in case of premature death
> (b) financial income support to the surviving person.

4. Amount of Insurance Needed

How much life insurance should one have? There is no precise mathematical answer to this question. An investment expert has said that one needs six to ten times one's annual income depending upon a person's individual needs and capacity to pay premiums. Thus, the benchmark can only be a reasonable estimate.

One way to assess one's financial worth is to calculate human life value, a concept propounded by Solomon S. Hubner, Wharton School of Business. *Human life value is the net present value of a person's potential future earnings over the rest of his working life span.* For this, you have to take into account your future earnings, the inflation rate, family expenses, taxation rates. Of course this is only a representative index. *The HLV concept works on the assumption that human life is an income generating asset.*

If a person aged 35 earns Rs. 3 lakhs a year and has a working life span of 25 years, his future gross earnings are Rs. 75/- lakhs. If we add 10 per cent rise in income every year, the gross expected earnings come to Rs. 2.5 crores. If 60 per cent of income goes for personal expenses and taxes the rest constitutes family expenses, which comes to Rs. 1.1 crore. If we assume an inflation rate at 3.5 per cent per year, the present value of Rs. 1.1 crore payable over a 25 years period, would be Rs. 46 lakhs, which is his financial worth to the family.

The next question to consider would be: whether one can afford to pay the premiums for this amount. One will have to take into account other commitments to savings, such as P.F.,PPF, NSCs, Mutual Fund, UTI etc.

HLV Model is thus only a broad model. It is less than a perfect model. It does not take into account a person's assets and liabilities such as long-term debts. It does not reflect dynamic real-life compulsions. Changes in life cycle, warrant periodic review of one's risk cover to ensure that one's risk cover keeps pace with changing needs of life. There are significant milestones in one's life that necessitate a review of one's life insurance needs. The critics of the HLV approach stress this point and state that one cannot have a mathematical solution to one's insurance needs. In Western countries, agents are relying more on the Needs approach, which takes into account the totality of a person's financial status.

One more model is called the Multiple Earnings Model which is simple to follow. One calculates amount of life insurance by multiplying one's gross earnings by 3.6 or even as high as 10. This model is thus only an approximation.

Ideally, one should combine the HLV approach with the Needs approach. Having decided upon an ideal amount of insurance cover, actual sale can be effected according to the present needs of the prospect.

Periodical review does not necessarily mean enhancing one's insurance periodically. If after a few years, one finds that there is no need to provide for dependents, one may consider closing down those policies, where premiums are quite high.

The underlying idea under all the three approaches is that of the life cycle. Tolstoy says in his famous novel, "War & Peace", "Life is like a flying wheel." Life can be divided into stages, layers or steps — one over another, but there are no clear dividing lines.

5. Broadly the life cycle or circle can be described by way of the following diagram.

Stage I
Newly born and young children. They are to be supported by parents. *No Insurance*

Stage II
Age 18-25 Single. Starts earning. May or may not have dependent parents/brethren
Personal Accident over small term insurance convertible

Stage III
Age 25-35
Gets married. Need to cover risk of death increases.
Term Insurance Convertible with Medical Insurance

Stage IV
Age 35-40
Has children, old parents/spouse may/may not be earning.
Additional Term cover plus Endowment 50 or 55 or 60 Deferred annuities for old age

Stage V
Age 40-50
May add personal assets such as house, vehicle for which *collateral/mandatory insurance* would be necessary
Decreasing Term Assurance, Fire Insurance. Auto Insurance and Health Insurance

Stage VII
Age 50-60
To review sufficiency of Insurance cover and other forms of savings. *Short term endowment and investment oriented plans may be necessary.*

Stage VII
Age 60 plus
Superannuation retirement age. He needs *Health, Personal accident, property, Insurance cover,* life insurance covers may not be available easily and may be very costly. Annuity payments start. *He can purchase more Immediate Annuities*

Wealth-Cycle Concept

The investment-oriented person looks at life as a wealth accumulation machine and not merely an income-earning machine. For this he breaks life into five stages.

The *first* stage is the *accumulation stage*. The goal-attainment is far away. You have to put your money into long-term wealth.

The *second stage* is the *transitional stage*, when the set-goals are not very far. For instance, a person who is about to retire at the age of 60 should plan his retirement strategy 5 to 10 years in advance keeping in view his present income, future family responsibilities, the condition of health of himself and his family members. If the children are about to go in for college education or attain marriageable age in the near future, anticipated expenses should be locked in short-term liquid assets.

The *third* stage is the *attainment stage*, when one enjoys the fruits of his savings. If someone wants 8 per cent returns, he will have to set aside 12 to 15 times the monthly income in retirement plans. Equities are a good defence against inflation, since in a rising market, these can be disposed off at short notice to satisfy one's current needs.

The *next* stage would be one of *balancing your investment portfolio*.

Finally, one may be in a stage of getting a large lump sum income at one stroke, such as on retirement or sale of assets. Before investing one has to study taxation aspects. Life Insurance provides the best answer in the form of Annuities.

While as a measure of investment, Life insurance may not rank high, it must be remembered that there is no investment like Life Insurance which combines risk with return. *There is no substitute for life insurance from this point of view.*

6. ***Type of Insurance*** needed by an individual. This will depend upon his personal needs — present as well as future, as discussed above. Broadly speaking, these would be as under:

Term Insurance covers death risk. *This is ideal for making provision for dependents.*

Whole Life Insurance: When the term coincides with one's whole life i.e., the sum assured will come to an end only on death, at any time, unlike Term Assurance, which covers death during the specified term only. Some insurers have provided that they will be paying whole life policy moneys on completion of age 100. LIC of India pays on completion of 80 years of age or 35 years term whichever is later.

Endowment Type Policies: Endowment Type Policies are issued for a fixed term, usually not going beyond 70 years of the life assured. The sum assured is payable on completion of the selected terms (called maturity) or death, if earlier. These are the most popular forms of insurance in India. A variation of this policy is *moneyback,* where a partial sum is paid periodically, called survival benefits. On maturity, the balance sum assured is paid. Death cover is however full throughout the term. *Joint life endowment* assurance policies are also issued on the lives of husband-wife or partners. Children's assurances are issued in the form of *Deferred Assurances,* where the risk would commence on child's attaining majority.

Annuities are useful for old age provisions. These are useful to those who do not have the benefit of employee pension or social security. These cover the risk of living too long. With the ageing of the population these are now becoming popular.

SELF-STUDY QUESTIONS

1. What were various risks to which primitive man was exposed?
2. Define Insurance. How does it operate?
3. Mention references to insurance in Kautilya's Arthashastra.
4. What were the factors that brought out insurance in focus.
5. Mention peculiarities of life insurance from the standpoint of death.
6. What are the risks to which human life is exposed?
7. Explain OYTA. How does it operate?
8. Explain how Term Assurance works.
9. Each life insurance policy satisfies a particular need. Explain.

10. Explain Maslow's Theory of Psychological Needs.
11. Describe classification of needs.
12. What do you understand by HLV approach?
13. Explain the Multiple Earning Model.
14. What is Needs Approach? How does the life cycle or circle move? How is it relevant for life insurance.
15. What do you understand by wealth cycle concept? Is it relevant for life insurance business? If so, in what respect?
16. Describe the basic types of life insurance?
17. State which type of insurance would ideally satisfy the following needs.
    (a) Family provision in case of early death.
    (b) Old age provision
    (c) Provision for dependants in case of death at any time.

KEYWORDS TO REMEMBER

Security	Needs — analysis
Uncertainty	Human life value
Mortality	Multiple earnings
Disability	Life-cycle
Level Premium	Whole-life
OYTA	Endowment
Term Assurance	Annuities

❑❑❑

2

Life Insurance—Contract

Objectives

To provide an understanding of the nature of the life insurance contract and its applications.

Lesson Objectives

To enable the students to understand:

(1) Distinguishing characteristics of a life insurance contract.

(2) Implications and significance of a Proposal Form Warranties.

(3) Various conditions and privileges applicable to a life policy.

INTRODUCTION

1. Life Insurance contracts are subject to the Law of Contract i.e., Indian Contract Act, 1872. Anson describes the law of contract as that brand of law which determines the circumstances in which a promise shall be legally binding on the person making it. It is an agreement enforceable at law made between two more persons, by which rights are acquired by one or more to certain acts or forbearance on the part of another or others.

Pollock defines it as 'any promise enforceable at law.'

A Contract may be simple or speciality. Simple contract must be supported by a consideration. It is oral or implied by the conduct of the parties. A speciality contract must be in writing and may be enforced for damages without consideration.

A Contingent Contract is a contract to do or not to do something if some event collateral to the contract does not happen.

An Indemnity Contract is one where one party promises to save the other from the loss caused to him by the conduct of himself, or by the conduct of any other person. *Insurance contracts are not contracts of indemnity,* but the principle of indemnity applies to insurance contracts, except to life and accident insurance contracts. Some contracts fall into two or more categories. An insurance contract is a contract of *uberimae fides* i.e., utmost good faith. *Insurance, apart from its special features, is a contract between the person seeking to be insured and the insurer* (Punjab High Court in *Laxmi Insurance Co. vs. Bibi Padmavathi* (1961 Punj.).[1]

It is *aleatory* in so far as it depends upon a contingency, which may or may not take place. It is *voluntary* as the parties act in good faith and enter into terms of contract. It is *executory* from the Insurer's side but executed from Insured's side, as soon as he pays the premium. It is *synallagmatic* because it imposes reciprocal obligations. It is *bilateral* since it is in the nature of a mutual agreement imposing upon each one reciprocal obligations. It is *conditional* since it depends upon compliance with certain conditions precedent and conditions subsequent. It is *personal* as the obligation to pay does not attach to the property.

2. The basic essential characteristics of the contract are *(a) offer and acceptance (b) capacity to contract (c) consideration (d) legality of object, (e) consent.*

. The Life Insurance contract is based on a written proposal form signed by the proposer. In most of the contracts the proposer and the person whose life is to be insured are one and the same person (own life proposal). Relying on the replies given to the various questions which are relevant, important and material to acceptance of the risk, the insurer i.e., the Insurance company enters into contract and accepts the risk. The facts on which insurance is granted are solely in the possession of one party to the contract i.e., the proposer himself. Moreover, the contractual obligations are to be performed by the Insurer only at a future time. The proposer, who subsequently becomes the insured also promises to pay premiums in future. *Thus, insurance is largely a contract of promises. The subject matter of an insurance contract is thus intangible* — not seen, touched or felt, unlike in a commercial contract where the product purchased is a tangible one — physically examinable. *In a commercial contract, therefore, the principle of Caveat Emptor (Let the buyer be aware) applies.* This is so because in a commercial contract, the product to be purchased is available for inspection. Hence, the buyer is supposed to have purchased the product with open eyes. In a Life Insurance contract, however the product to be purchased and sold is the insured person himself. The facts which would affect the mortality (rate of dying) (in life insurance) or probability of loss (in general insurance), are in the possession of the proposer. The insurance company, the Insurer, may not be able to find out or locate adverse factors pertaining to personal history of accidents, injuries, sicknesses, hospitalisations, inspite of the best medical examination. Similarly, adverse family history may not be known unless the proposer himself discloses it. Even the agent who would have booked the proposal may not be in the know of things. Hence the duty cast on the proposer is great. *The law has recognised this as a principle of utmost good faith (Uberima fides).* The positive duty imposed on the proposer applies to all classes of insurance. In a life insurance contract, *the duty to disclose starts with the process of filling the proposal form and ends with the issue of First Premium Receipt (F.P.R.) by the Insurer.* This duty gets revived at the time of revival of a lapsed policy, reinstatement of a surrendered policy or of a foreclosed policy. *This duty to disclose is a positive duty and encompasses all the questions and answers contained in the proposal form.*

The statements made in the proposal form if wrong or untrue, amount to misstatement. Hence, if the proposer conceals some fact knowing it to be material, it is a fraud. Even without knowledge such concealment of material matter vitiates the contract (*Major Chopra vs. New Zealand Insurance Co.* (1967. Cal.) While Sec. 16 of Sale of Goods Act does not impose any implied condition or warranty as to the quality or fitness of the product, under insurance contract, there is an implied condition about disclosure of all material facts. *Hence, Insurance contracts are termed as contracts of utmost good faith.*

3. The statements made in the proposal form are in the nature of representations which should be substantially true. *The warranties, on the other hand are statements by which the assured undertakes that some particular thing shall or shall not be done or that some condition shall be fulfilled, or whereby he affirms or negatives the existence of a particular fact.* This definition has been given in Sec. 35 of the Marine Insurance Act, 1963. The Act further provides that a warranty is a condition which must be exactly complied with, whether it be material to the risk or not. Warranty, in the ordinary commercial parlance, merely means an undertaking or promise which is incidental or collateral to the main contract and hence it is not that important. In case of the breach of such promise, the aggrieved party can claim damages.

4. A warranty in a policy of life insurance is not collateral but basic to the contract. It amounts to a condition in any other contract and must be thoroughly complied with. The aggrieved party can repudiate the liability under the contract. In such an event materiality is not important. Lack of knowledge may not change the situation. The other party might not be put to any loss. *A warranty is incorporated in the policy, a representation is not.*

5. In a life insurance proposal, the proposer gives a declaration at the end of the proposal form, declaring that the statements in proposal form are entirely true and any untrue averment would entitle the insurer to set aside the contract and forfeit the payment made towards such contract. *Such declaration converts the representations into warranties.* This practice of Indian life assurance companies was stated in New

India vs. TSR Reddy. (1961-AP).[3] This situation has been confirmed in many subsequent pronouncements of the courts. English courts have also confirmed this view. Joel vs. Law Union Crown[4] Insurance (1908 KB); Godfrey vs. Britannic Assurance Co. (1963-SJ)[5] *Allahabad High Court has held that the declarations made in the proposal form amount to warranty and form the basis of the policy* (Brahma Dutt Sharma vs. LIC 1966 All).[6] In an earlier case All India General Insurance Co. Ltd. vs. S.P. Maheshwari (1960 All)[7] *non-disclosure of material facts was taken as a sufficient ground for repudiation.*

6. This right to repudiate is not however absolute. *Sec. 45 of Indian Insurance Act 1938 severely limits the freedom given to insurance companies in this regard.*

> This section does not apply to policies for two years. However, once the two years period is over, the Insurer, in order to repudiate any liability under a life insurance policy, must establish on the basis of written evidence that (1) the statements were inaccurate or false (2) such statement was on material matter or suppressed facts it was material to disclose (3) that the statement was fraudulently made (4) the policyholder knew at the time of making the statement that it was his duty to disclose.

The burden of proof is on the insurer. The proof must be shown. Mere constructive fraud will not suffice. (LIC vs. Parvativardhini Amma 1965, Madras)[8]. The Doctrine of Warranty therefore does not apply after a period of two years. The words "The date on which it was effected means the date on which contract is effected. The case of antedating or backdating of the risk for personal convenience will not be covered by it. If it is allowed, the very purpose of Sec. 45 would be defeated. (Khamele vs. LIC, 1971 Bom.)[9] In case of revival of a lapsed policy, 2 years period is to be counted from the original date of commencement, the section applies even if the life assured had died within two years of the commencement of the policy. The date of the repudiation letter is important (Vaid Mahesh Shastri vs. LIC (1968 Cal.).[10] Materiality is a question of fact and would embrace every circumstance that would affect the decision of a prudent underwriter — in deciding whether he will accept the risk and, if so on what terms. (Major V.S. Chopra vs. New Zealand Insurance Co. 1967 Cal.)[11]

7. Sec. 45 of the Insurance Act has placed certain restrictions on the common law's right to repudiate an insurance policy under certain circumstances. *The statutory provisions thus make a life insurance policy indisputable once the two years period from F.P.R. is over.* The two years period is to be computed from the date of F.P.R. to the date of repudiation. Moreover Sec. 45 does not mention the word 'Death' at all. Thus, the *Insurer can proceed in respect of a policy which is in force, if it has evidence to prove that the particular policy was obtained by non-disclosure of material facts.*

8. Thus the proposal form as the basis of the contract assumes great significance in a life insurance contract. The agent's Confidential Report helps the underwriter to decide whether the life proposed is insurable and if so on what terms. The Agent is the person who has met the proposer in person. He would have enquired about his financial status as also possible moral hazard. *Hence, the agent is called the first line underwriter or primary underwriter.* Barring a few cases of small sums assured on the lives of young persons, a good many proposers are secured under medical examination which is to be carried out by a Medical Examiner appointed by the Insurer for this purpose. The practice is to have a panel of Medical Examiners, to whom the Agent should take his prospect for carrying out the medical examination. Panels would be prepared for general practitioners for carrying out clinical medical examination and also for specialists like cardiologists, radiologists, pathologists etc. The medical examiner has to report on the proposer's present medical status based on his height, weight, chest and abdomen measurements, systolic-diastolic blood pressure readings, pulse rate, specific gravity of urine, conditions of eyes, teeth, hearing, presence or absence of small pox or vaccination marks etc. The purpose of the medical examination is to assist the underwriter to decide whether the present medical status of the proposer entitles him to a normal policy or not. It helps him in arriving at the

Extra Mortality Rating on account of personal condition of the proposer. It also helps him to decide whether any additional special reports are necessary. Thus, though *the medical report is not the basis of the contract, it is the basis of the underwriting.*

9. When the proposal is accepted and the full first premium alongwith the consent letter wherever necessary, is received, the insurer issues the F.P.R., which shows that the company has gone on risk. This is followed by the issue of the policy document which is the evidence of a contract.

Construction of a Life Insurance Policy: The interpretation of a policy document is to be done as expressed by the parties themselves. Where, however there is a doubt about the interpretation of a particular word, phrase or a clause, the one favourable to the insured would be preferred, because the policy document is prepared by the insurer and the insured had no say in the arrangement of these words or phrases. This rule of construction against the insurer and favourable to the insured rests on the maxim *contra preferentum.* However, this rule is to be applied if other rules fail to interpret the construction. (Laxmi Insurance vs. Bibi Padmavati 1961 Punj.)

10. The insurers follow a practice of standard form of policies for various plans of insurance, with standardised policy conditions and privileges. It has a standard schedule which gives details of policy, standard preamble and a standard declaration of the contract Any modifications in this policy will have to be done by a separate clause or endorsements which shall be attached to the policy and this is considered as a part of the policy. Therefore any mistake in the drafting of the clause/endorsement will be construed against the Insurer.

In LIC vs. Dharamvir Anand (SC 1998)[12] a proposal on the life of a minor girl was accepted with clause 4(b) which stated that at any time after the date of commencement of the risk but before the expiry of three years from the date of the policy if the Life Assured committed suicide LIC's liability was limited to refund of the premium. The District Consumer's Forum, State Commission and National Commission ruled in favour of the proposer, but the Supreme Court reversed this decision and ruled in favour of LIC. This case also confirms the view that the risk commences from the date of FPR and not from the date of commencement of the policy which can be backdated.

11. Section 2(36) of the Companies Act defines the term Prospectus, which is applicable to the companies incorporated under the Act, However, the Insurance Act 1938 does not define the prospectus. Under Sec. 3 of the Insurance Act every application for registration shall be accompanied by a certified copy of published prospectus, if any. IRDA (Registration of Companies) Regulations 2000 - Sec. 2(9) uses the same words. Thus apparently, publishing of prospectus is not essential for Registration. Section 119 provides for inspection and supply of copies of published prospectus. If the life assured relies on the prospectus published by the insurer, though the prospectus is not referred to in the policy, it can be taken as a part of the contract (Sun Life of Canada vs. Jervis (1943 All).[11] But the prospectus will not be relied on for the interpretation of the contract, which is a document by itself. Sun Life vs. Nilratan Mukerjee (1938, Cal)[14]

12. Delivery of the policy document is to be made to the proposer and the life assured, if he is one and the same person and to the proposer, if he is different from the life assured. The policy is to be delivered against proper record and identification. Normal practice is to send it by Registered Post acknowledgement due. It may be delivered through Authorised Person/Representative.

13. Policy conditions and provisions: *A life insurance policy expresses the terms of contract between the insurer and the insured.* The policy document should reveal (i) the definition of the risk covered, (ii) the duration of the risk, (iii) the premium, and (iv) the amount of insurance (Ref. Law of Insurance Macgillvary). The policy, however, states rights and privileges of the insured person and his obligations as well. The policy documents will have standardised and printed conditions. Any variation will be provided by suitable endorsements placed on the policy. These conditions are of three types.

(i) Conditions which explain the nature of the contract e.g. proof of age and assignment.

(ii) Conditions which add to or enhance the scope of the contract. e.g., Non-forfeiture Regulations, Accident and Disability Benefits.

(iii) Conditions which limit the scope of the contract. e.g. loan and suicide.

14. Proof of Age: The premium depends upon the mortality relevant to the age. Mortality depends upon age. The higher the age, higher the mortality, hence higher the premium. The insurers, therefore insist on admission of age at the time of issuing the policy. However, if for some reasons, age remains to be admitted or the age already admitted proves to be wrong, the insurer has a right to make necessary adjustments in the terms and benefits offered under the plan. If the age proves lower, difference in premiums will be refunded without interest. However, if the age proves higher, the policyholder has to pay arrears of premium with specified rate of interest. The insurer has a right to adjust the plan — term, sum assured, mode of payment of premium, benefits etc. on the basis of the correct age admitted. This right can be exercised at any time during the currency of the policy, including payment at maturity/death claim. Indisputability envisaged by Sec. 45 of the Insurance Act does not apply to admission of age. The proviso to Section 45 clearly provides for and recognises the insurer's rights to adjust policy benefits for understatement of age, even beyond 2 years' period, without proving ingredients of Sec. 45. This is so because, age is material to acceptance of life risk.

15. Days of Grace: The insurance contract consists of promises made by both parties, insurer and insured. If there is a breach of promise, the contract would be affected. If the insured does not pay due premiums on time, policy may get lapsed or may become paid up for reduced sum assured. The insurer is not under obligation to send Renewal Notice to the insured but he sends it as a matter of courtesy. As a rule premium should be paid on or before due date. But the insurance companies grant 30 days of grace i.e., period beyond the due date during which the premium can be paid without any penalty and the death risk cover continues during this period. If death takes place during this period, the full sum assured becomes payable, subject to recovery of unpaid premiums with interest upto date of death. Period of 30 days has to be calculated from the date next to the due date. (T.G. Rajan vs. Asiatic).[15] If the policy is in force for a period of 3 years, the days of grace get extended to a period of 6 months from the date of the first unpaid premium. If the premiums are paid for at least 5 years, the grace period is extended to one year from the date of first unpaid premium (FUP). *These are called claims' concession and extended claims' concession respectively.*

16. Lapse and Revival: Where the premium is not paid on the due date or within the days of grace, the policy lapses but it can be revived at any time during the remaining period of the policy, subject to medical evidence and arrears of premium along with interest thereon at the applicable rate. If the policy has lapsed within 3 years of the date of commencement it is not entitled to any claims' concession, except days of grace, usually 30 days. Statistics of policies lapsed or forfeited have to be mentioned in form DDD to be submitted to IRDA. Both the policies whether lapsed without acquiring surrender value or lapsed after acquiring surrender value can be revived in the manner as stated above. There are various types of revival schemes. Simple revival consists of payment of arrears of premiums with interest thereon at an appropriate rate of interest, as specified by the insurer. This scheme is applicable if not more than six months have elapsed since the date of First Unpaid Premium. In other words the policy must not be in a lapsed state for more than six months.

The Ordinary Revival Scheme, consists of obtaining the aforesaid requirement alongwith a medical report. If the sum assured is not large and if the original proposal had been accepted under a Non-medical scheme i.e. without medical report, insurer may proceed on the basis of a simple declaration of good health.

If the lapsation period is long, the arrears of premiums could be a very substantial amount, the insurer offers a Loan-cum-Revival scheme, provided the policy has acquired surrender value, notionally on the date of revival. Insurance Act, 1938 Sec. 113 provides for acquiring of paid up value and guaranteed surrender value, if at least three years' premiums have been paid under the policy. Special surrender value can be calculated by multiplying notional paid-up value, which is calculated on the assumption that all the premiums have been paid up-to-date, by appropriate special surrender value factor, which is a function of the duration elapsed to the total term of the policy. In case of a with-Profit policy, bonuses accrued upto the date of First Unpaid Premium (no bonuses accrue for the part of the yearly premium paid but for the full completed years) on the full sum assured are added to the paid-up value so calculated. This notional loan amount is utilised towards arrears of premium with interest thereon. If some difference falls due for payment to the policyholder, the same would be refunded. If some balance is due from him the same is to remitted by him. The cost of the loan bond stamp paper will have to be borne by the policy holder who will have to continue to pay loan-interest along with the premiums.

If the policy is a Money-Back type, the Survival Benefit falling due for payment, periodically, can be deemed to be notionally due which can be utilised for adjusting arrears of premium with interest thereon.

If the policy is not eligible for loan or survival benefit, and the arrears of premium are a sizeable amount, *revival by instalments* can be considered. The policyholder, in that case, can pay arrears of premium by suitable instalments, which should be paid alongwith regular premiums. *The unpaid instalments of premiums are treated as a debt/charge against the policy.*

If the policy was in force for at least six months but had not acquired surrender value, *Special Revival is considered*. In this case the original date of commencement of the policy is shifted by the period for which policy was in force. A fresh policy will have to be issued for the age as on that date. The arrears of premiums will be a nominal amount. The cost of the preparation of the policy will have to be borne by the policyholder.

Revival constitutes a new contract, a novatio, but for the purpose of Sec. 45 of the Insurance Act, the period of two years is to be calculated from the date on which it was originally effected (Mithoo Lal Nayak vs. LIC, SC. 1962)[16]

17. Paid up and Surrender: These are two distinct benefits/ privileges available to a policy holder, who keeps his policy in force for at least three years. Sec. 113 grants this benefit. If the premiums for at least three years have been paid, the policy acquires a guaranteed surrender value, which is at least 30% of the premiums paid, excluding first year's premium and excluding extra premiums paid, if any. The insurance company however grants a more liberal surrender value on the basis of multiplying accrued paid-up value by appropriate surrender value factor (Please also refer para 2 above).

18. Loans: The insurer grants loan @ 90% of the special surrender value on in-force policies and 85% of the special surrender value on paid-up policies. For this purpose policy under grace period is treated as in-force policy. The loan so granted need not be repaid since it is secured by the surrender value. However, if loan interest, which is to be paid on half yearly basis, whatever may be the mode of payment of premium, is outstanding under a paid-up policy for more than a year, the Insurer, as the creditor has a right to take foreclosure action. This consists of adjusting the outstanding loan and interest from the surrender value available under the policy. Such a foreclosed policy can be reinstated within 6 months of foreclosure if medical evidence satisfactory to the insurer is produced, alongwith the repayment of loan amount and arrears of premium with interest, if any.

19. Paid-up Value is acquired if payments of premiums is stopped after paying them for at last three years. Paid-up value is the reduced sum assured calculated on a proportionate basis, which number of premiums paid bears to the number of premiums payable. Once the policy is made paid-up, it ceases to participate in future profits (bonuses) that may be declared by the company. If the life assured dies at any time during the remaining term of the policy (after the expiry of days of grace are over), the paid-up policy is payable in accordance with the terms and conditions of the original policy. Section 113 of the Insurance Act provides for paid-up value and guaranteed surrender value.

20. Maturity: If all the premiums under the policy are paid, the policy matures for payment on the date of maturity e.g., a twenty-years Endowment policy taken on 1.6.1983 matures on 1.6.2003. The policy continues to be in force upto 12 p.m. on 1.6.2003. Death at any time before that time means that there is a death claim under the policy. *The liability under a maturity claim and death claim may not be the same.*

The requirements for the settlement of a maturity claim are (1) Original policy document for cancellation or endorsement (2) Completed and signed Discharge Voucher (3) A simple claim form duly completed and signed by the claimant.

If the policy is assigned in favour of a third party in terms of Section 38 of the Insurance Act, the claim requirements will have to be complied with by the assignee and the claim amount will have to be settled in his favour. If the policy is assigned in favour of wife as a Trustee under Sec. 6 of the Married Women's Property Act, the claim will have to be settled in the wife's favour. The same applies if the official assignee sends a notice of his interest in the policy. If a notice under Sec. 226 of the Income Tax Act is received, the assured should be advised to get the notice vacated. ITO has to be informed that under the Civil Procedure Code, moneys under life insurance policy can be attached only when these fall due i.e., on the date of maturity.

In the case of Money-Back plans, survival benefits fall periodically. These are to be settled after following the above procedure. However, there are some minor differences. The policy document is to be sent back to the claimant after endorsing the policy, to the effect that the survival benefit has been paid. If the survival benefit amount is small, say upto Rs. 20,000/-, this procedure may be waived and the payment released.

If the policyholder dies after the date of maturity, but before encashing the maturity cheque already sent to him, it is nonetheless a maturity claim. The nominee under Section 39 of Insurance Act has no right whatsoever, to receive the policy moneys. He/she may join as one of the heirs. In case of Money Back type of policy, only the balance sum assured would be payable on maturity, along with accrued bonuses on full sum assured.

21. Nomination is a creation of Insurance Act, 1938. Sec. 39 of this Act provides that *a person holding a policy on his own life can nominate a person to receive the policy moneys in case of policyholder's death during the term of the policy.* Nominee has no right, present or future, in the policy moneys. If the nominee is minor the policyholder may name an appointee to receive policy moneys during the minority of the nominee. *Nominee is merely a trustee of the policy moneys.* If there is more than one nominee, they may take the claim as tenants-in-common and not as joint-tenants. Since the nominee has no title, he cannot pass any title to his successors. Successive nomination is however permissible. Sec. 39(2) provides that nomination can be cancelled by an endorsement or a Will, Sec. 39(4) states that nomination is cancelled by a transfer or assignment of a policy. Sec 39(5) provides that where a policy matures for payment during the life time of the policy holder, the amount secured by the policy shall be payable to the policyholder himself.

Sec. 39(6) provides that the nominee does not acquire any title to the policy money where a policy matures for payment or on death of the policyholder. Nomination to be effectual must be incorporated in the text of the policy or if it is incorporated by endorsement, it must be communicated to the insurer and registered by him. If the nominee is minor, appointment of a major person should be made. Sec. 39(b) provides for payment of policy moneys to surviving nominees. Hence distinct shares cannot be specified. Nomination does not divest the life assured of his rights in the policy and he retains disposing powers. Subsequent assignment cancels nomination and the same cannot be revived merely on reassignment. A fresh nomination has to be made, otherwise title remains open.

22. Assignment of a life insurance policy is governed by Sec. 38 of the Insurance Act and not by Sec. 130 of Transfer of Property Act, though moneys payable under a life insurance policy is an actionable claim. Sec. 38(1) sets the procedure for assignment. This is to be done by a separate instrument or by an endorsement on the policy itself by the transferor or assignor. Sec. 38(2) states that the assignment is complete and effectual on execution duly attested. A notice in writing should be served on the insurer alongwith the instrument or a copy thereof.

Sec. 38(3) states that the receipt of notice shall determine the priority of claims. Insurer has to register the assignment and acknowledge it (Sec. 38A)

Sec. 38(5) clarifies that the transferee is subject to all liabilities and equities to which the transferor was subject. He can institute legal proceedings without transferor's consent. Sec. 38(7) recognises conditional assignment.

Thus, Sec. 38 creates two types of assignments — absolute and conditional. Assignment has to be for valuable consideration. But if it is for natural love and affection, no consideration is necessary. Loan cannot be granted under a policy subject to conditional assignment, except assignment in favour of the insurer for this very purpose. Assignment of a part of policy moneys is not permissible.

23. Suicide, that is killing oneself by one's own hands, is excluded for a period of one year from the date of F.P.R. This one year's period is not counted from the date of commencement. Under English Law, suicide while sane, is a crime, suicide while of unsound mind is not a crime. In India suicide is not a crime, attempt to commit is. The claim is admissible only after a period of one year from the date of suicide. While nothing is payable under the policy, *bonafide* interests of the third party are protected, provided notice in writing is received by the insurer at least 30 days before suicide. *Suicide is not an accident. Hence, Double Accident Claim is not admissible at any time.* Since suicide is unnatural death, though not an accident there would be Police Report Panchanama, FIR, Post Mortem Report, etc. available. This may reveal information which may affect the basic contract itself, in a few cases. However, for repudiation of the liability, insurer will have to prove non-disclosure of material facts independently on the basis of written evidence e.g., previous history of depression, or other mental disorder earlier attempt to commit suicide, or family history of suicide etc. and its non-disclosure in the proposal form.

24. Death Claims: Most of the life insurance policies provide for payment of sum assured on the death of the life assured taking place. This is provided by the term insurance portion of the policy. Under some policies a double or triple sum assured is payable on death within the term of the policy. Some policies provide for reduced sum assured for the extended period usually ten years beyond the term of the policy without collecting any premium for the extended term.

While maturity claim intimations are sent by the insurer himself on the basis of computer-generated records for the whole year, death claim intimations must be received from the near and dear ones of the deceased life assured. If the intimation is received from a stranger, enquiries should be made, about his relationship with the deceased life assured.

If the death claim intimation is received after 3 years from the date of death, the claim is barred by Limitations Act 1963, Sec 44(a). If the claim is repudiated, the period of limitation starts from such repudiation/denial.

25. For consideration of a death claim, the following requirements are to be complied with:

(1) Proof of death — from Public Death Register. In exceptional circumstances like air or ship accidents where the dead body is not traceable, alternative proof of death such as airline's or ship master's certificate may be accepted. In cases where dead body is carried away by a wild animal or a crocodile, a police report will have to be obtained.

(2) As already discussed, proof of age is necessary if the age was not already admitted.

(3) Original policy document: If it was lost, a duplicate might already have been issued.

(4) Proof of Title. If there is no subsisting nomination or assignment or trust, proof of title of the claimant will have to be produced. The claimant will have to declare the status under which he is claiming the policy moneys — as nominee, assignee, trustee, legatee or heir. Last medical attendant's

certificate is necessary in case of natural deaths. In case of unnatural deaths, such as suicide, murder, accident, certified copies of police investigation report and post-mortem reports would be necessary. The purpose is to establish fact of death and the identity of the person.

26. Presumption of Death: Under Section 108 of the Indian Evidence Act, 1872, if it is proved that the person has not been heard of for seven years by those who would have naturally heard of him had he been alive, the presumption of law is that he is dead. Hence, if the policyholder is missing for seven years, his heirs can apply to the appropriate civil court and get a court order declaring that the life assured might be presumed to be dead. A claim is payable if the policy is in force or in a paid-up condition, as on the date of the court's order. The exact date and time of death is not a matter of presumption but of active proof. Therefore, in the absence of any such proof, the date of the court's order could be taken as the Date of Death. Policy moneys would be payable as per policy status as on date of the court order.

The death claim amount would be payable to nominee/ assignee/trustee under MWP Act, or in the absence of these, to legal heirs of the deceased person, who should submit to the insurer proper proof of representative title – from an appropriate court – in the form of a probate or letters of administration to the estate of the deceased, or a certificate granted under Administrator General's Act 1913, or a succession certificate. The moneys payable under a life insurance policy after the death of the life assured constitutes a conditional and contingent debt.

SELF-STUDY QUESTIONS

1. Describe the various types of contracts.
2. What are the essentials of a valid agreement. How far do these apply to life insurance?
3. Discuss the principle of *caveat emptor* and *uberimae fides*.
4. What points must be proved by the insurer to repudiate its liability (1) Within 2 years (2) after 2 years of FPR. Why is the agent called "primary underwriter."

5. Write short notes on
   (a) Rule of construction.
   (b) Legal status of prospectus
   (c) Days of Grace
   (d) Claims concessions
6. Describe different methods of revival.
7. Distinguish between:
   (a) Guaranteed S.V. and Special S.V.
   (b) Conditional and Absolute assignments
8. Describe the procedure for the settlement of a maturity claim.
9. Bring out the difference between nomination and assignment.
10. What are the requirements for consideration of claim?
11. How do insurers deal with suicide as one of the policy conditions?
12. When can a presumption of death be made?

KEY WORDS

Insurable Interest: Utmost good faith. Materiality; Non-disclosure; Breach of warranty; Days of Grace; Nomination, Assignment; Presumption of death.

❑❑❑

3 Life Insurance — Risk

Objectives

To provide an in-depth understanding of the factors affecting measurement of risk.

Lesson Objectives
To enable the students to understand:
(1) Factors governing sum assured.
(2) Measurement of risk and mortality.
(3) Treatment of sub-standard lives.
(4) Elements of underwriting including calculation of premium and HLV approach.
(5) Creation and utilisation of surplus, life fund and payment of bonus.

1. Sum Assured: Under a life insurance contract, an agreed sum called *sum assured* becomes payable, if the insured event takes place in the manner as stated in the policy.

The insurer charges appropriate premium to cover the risk involved. Since *premium is the price charged for covering risk, on human life, it must be sufficient to cover the cost of risk involved.* In life insurance, the product insured is 'human life'. It is quite difficult to judge accurately the exact cost of risk involved. Therefore a tool is developed to arrive at the chance of death of survival at various ages. It is called a mortality table. This represents experience of assured lives who have been insured for one year or more with the insurer. Mortality denotes rate of dying at a particular age for a period of one year. Mortality would differ from person to person, year to year and also as between male and female. Mortality cannot be studied for a day or two. It has to be studied for a long period. The group of persons to be studied should be sufficiently large, so that it can be subject to law of large numbers. This is also known as *Bernouli's Theorem. This states that the larger the number of separate risks of a like nature forming one group, the less uncertainty will be there as to the amount of expected loss within a given period. In other words, the larger the number of studied observations, the more accurate will be the estimates worked on that basis.*

An example can clarify this point. A coin is tossed and it falls on the ground. A coin has two sides, head and tail. Thus a coin can show-up two sides, but only one side at a time. The probability of either head or tail showing up is ½ i.e., 50%. This probability will hold good provided the coin is tossed a large number of times. Reverting to life insurance, we can say insuring an individual or two would be a gamble, but *if we insure a large group or persons, we would be in a position to predict with a near accuracy the probability of a member of that group dying within a period of one year. This is called rate of mortality, which is always age specific and time-specific*. This is so because persons of the same age are exposed to the same degree of mortality (probability of dying within a year).

2. Mortality Tables are prepared on the basis of study of assured lives for a period of time, usually 3 to 5 years. At every age deaths take place. These are tabulated showing rate of dying and rate of surviving (complementary probability) for every year.

A typical mortality table would appear like this:

1961-64 OM TABLE

Age at the beginning of the year	*No. of living at the beginning of the year*	*No. of death during the year*	*Yearly probability of death*	*Yearly probability of surviving*
1	*2*	*3*	*4*	*5*
35	9,79,217	1410	.00144	.99856
36	9,77,807	1535	.00157	.99843
37	9,76,272	1679	.00172	.99828
38	9,74,593	1842	.00189	.99811
39	9,72,751	2033	.00209	.99791
40	9,70,718	2242	.00231	.99769
41	9,68,476	2479	.00256	.99744
42	9,65,997	2743	.00284	.99716
43	9,63,254	3044	.00316	.99684
44	9,60,210	3370	.00351	.99633
45	9,56,840	3732	.00390	.99610

This Table shows that the chance of dying the at age of 35 is .00144, it increases to .00390 at the age of 45. The last column shows the probability of survival. These probabilities of death and survival are made use of in arriving *at the mathematical value of the risk* for lives belonging to a group whose experience may be expected to more or less compare favourably with the mortality table. If it happens, one can say that the premiums charged are adequate to meet the risk involved. In other words mortality experience is satisfactory.

3. Risk Premium for One Year Term Assurance *is the product of the chance of probability of death during the year and the sum assured.* The evaluation of the risk premium is based on the mathematical probability of the event happening. The larger the number of lives assured the closer should be the amount of claims to the amount of premiums received.

As in general insurance, life insurance contracts can be arranged on a year to year basis. This system which was tried in the earlier years of modern life assurance business had to be given up for its drawbacks. In the first instance, if the health of the person deteriorates, the insurer may charge a higher rate of premium or may deprive him of the insurance cover next year. On the other hand, a person who is in excellent health may not renew the contract. Even those who want to renew the contract, may have to renew the same with higher premium because of higher age. There would also be *a tendency on the part of the not so good lives (under-average lives) to 20 in for insurance on a large scale. Such a tendency is called Adverse selection.* The life insurer has to exercise great care in avoiding adverse selection. If this is not checked, the premiums collected may not prove adequate to meet the cost of the claims. Hence, the insurer has to *select* the lives, *assess* the risk on the available data, *classify* it on the basis of degree of under-averageness and *charge suitable extra premium or use some other method to take care of the extra risk involved. This is called 'underwriting'.*

The system of charging increasing premium every year is called assessmentism. The premium that is charged should be adequate to meet the mortality for that age. As the mortality, increases with age, the premium increases with it. It may become prohibitive at higher ages. Hence, an alternative was found by charging a level premium which would be the mathematical equivalent of the single premium required for granting a fixed-term Term insurance.

This can be projected on a Graph.

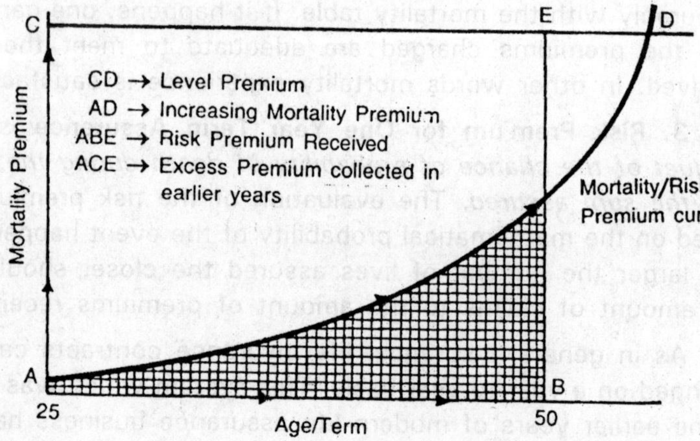

This level premium tends to be higher than risk premium in the early years of the policy. The burden of heavier premiums in later years is shifted to these earlier years. In these earlier years, premiums received exceed the amount of premiums required in earlier years. This excess is invested in accordance with legislative guidelines to earn interest. Thus, this excess goes on accumulating with interest. *Individually, it is a 'Policy Reserve' which actually represents Policy Liability. Cumulatively it constitutes a 'Life Fund' which gets enhanced by accretion of premiums received and interest earned and gets depleted by claims, commissions, salaries and other expenses.* If the company maintains its *solvency*, the Life Fund steadily goes on increasing. Since it is available in the form of various assets, both should match to a large extent. e.g. LIC's total Life Fund as on 31.3.02 was Rs. 2,27,009 crores, while its assets amounted to Rs. 2,45,331 crores. The two sources of income of any life insurance company are premiums and interest. For LICI, these figures were Rs. 48,963.60 crores and Rs. 22,695.42 crores respectively as on 31.3.02.

The insurers therefore rightly pass on a share of interest earnings to the policyholders by reducing the premium amount. At the same time the policyholder should bear his share of expenses which are necessarily to be incurred for running the life insurance business.

4. Thus, we start with **Risk Premium** which is sufficient to cover the mortality for a given age for a period of one year. When adjusted for interest, it becomes *Net Premium*. After loading it with expenses, it becomes *office premium*. Finally the actuary makes provisions for Bonus Loadings in respect of with-profit policies. Provision is also made for inflation, which reduces the value of premiums receivable and the claims payable in future. The final outcome is *Tabular Premium*, which is quoted in company's Tables of Premium Rates.

Life insurance contracts are long term contracts. Hence, an actuary has to take into account any possible loss in investments due to fluctuations in interest rates as also loss on some investments. *The higher the interest rate assumed, the lower would be the premium.*

5. Expenses incurred by the insurer may be classified as follows:

(1) Expenses connected with selling of new policies, underwriting and issue of new policies such as agents' commission, medical fees, Development staff salaries, New business staff salaries, advertisement and publicity, cost of preparing new policies, stamp duty etc.

(2) Expenses connected with servicing of policies — including cost of servicing claims.

(3) General expenses including valuation expenses.

(4) Expenses connected with investment of funds.

Broadly these are categorised as new business expenses and renewal expenses.

These expenses may vary (a) with the annual premium, e.g., commission, (b) with the number of policies, e.g. policy preparation costs, (c) with the sum assured e.g. medical fees, stamp duty and cost of underwriting decision. The basic premiums are calculated on a yearly basis per thousand sum assured. If the mode of payment is yearly or half-yearly, a small reduction in tabular premium, as a certain percentage of premium, is allowed. This is called mode rebate. If the sum assured is large, incidence of fixed costs which do not vary with the sum assured goes down. Hence, large Sum Assured Rebate is allowed from the Tabular Premium.

It is possible to merge these rebates in the tabular premium itself so that no separate rebates be allowed while calculating the instalment premium, which can be on yearly, half-yearly, quarterly or monthly basis, according to the option of the policyholders.

6. Risk Premium: The mortality table relating to experience of assured lives of LIC during 1970-73 is known as LIC (1970-73) Mortality Table. According to this table the number of deaths expected to occur within any year out of 1,00,000 lives of a given age are as under.

Age	Expected No. of deaths
20	130
25	128
30	134
35	178
40	280
45	465
50	772
55	1258
60	2014
65	3165

If 1,00,000 persons aged 30 are insured for a period of one year, one would expect 134 death claims, if (1970-73) assured lives experience holds good. If the sum assured is Rs. 1,00,000, the expected liability would be Rs. 1,34,000/- and the contribution from each would be Rs. 1.34. This is the risk premium payable by persons, each person being insured for Rs. 1,00,000/- at age 30. We have already studied this aspect.

Restated: *The mathematical value of the Risk Premium for a one year term assurance is equal to the product of the rate of mortality and the sum assured.* (interest income ignored for the time being). The Risk Premium thus goes on increasing from Re. 1.34 at age 30 to Rs. 31.63 at age 65. A further mortality investigation was done during 1975-79 and new mortality tables called LIC (1975-79) Ultimate Mortality table was formed and LIC revised its premium rates w.e.f. 1.4.80.

7. Interest: *is the price paid for the use of money.* When the money is invested, the person who uses the money pays interest to the lender. Interest earned each year earns interest in the subsequent years. *When interest earned earns additional interest, it is called compound interest.* An amount of Re.1/- will accumulate at the rate of 3% per annum compound interest at the end of one year, two years etc. to 1.03000, 1.6090 and so on. At 6% rate of interest, it would become 1.06000, 1.12360 etc. Conversely, if we find out what amount will accumulate to Re.1/- at the end of one year, two years etc. at 3% or 6% compound interest, we get sums of .97087, .94260 and .94340, .89000 and so on. The present value of one rupee at 3% per annum compound interest at the end of 5 years is Rs. .86261. The present value of Rs. 1,000 at the end of 5 years would be Rs. 1,000 x .86261 = Rs. 862.61. This means that if we invest Rs. 862.61 now at 3% per annum compound interest at the end of 5 years this would amount to Rs. 1,000/-.

From the (1961-64) mortality table quoted above if 979217 persons of age 35 go in for a Temporary Assurance for a period of 10 years and if we expect them to follow the same pattern as displayed by this table, we have to expect 1410 deaths at age 35, 1535 at 36 and so on. If we assume that Rs. 1,000/- would be the sum assured payable on death, the cost of insurance at the end of one, two three... ten years would be 1410/979217 x Rs. 1,000, 1535/979217 x Rs. 1,000, 1679/979217 x Rs. 1,000 .... 3370/979217 x Rs. 1,000. Present value of Re. 1/- to be received at the end of the year at 3% per annum and 6% per annum.

End of the year	*@ 3%*	*@ 6%*
1.	.97087	.94340
2.	.94260	.89000
3.	.91514	.83962
4.	.88849	.79209
5.	.86261	.74726
6.	.83748	.70496
7.	.81309	.66506
8.	.78941	.62741
9.	.76642	.59190
10.	.74409	.55839

We assume that the claims would be payable at the end of the year. The present value of each probability of death in case of ten years' assurance will be @ 3% as follows:

1st year's insurance to provide for death between 35 and 36

$$\frac{1410}{979217} \times 1,000 \times .97087 = 1.398$$

2nd year's insurance to provide for death between 36 and 37

$$\frac{1535}{979217} \times 1{,}000 \times .94260 = 1.478$$

3rd year's insurance to provide for death between 37 and 38

$$\frac{1679}{979217} \times 1{,}000 \times .91514 = 1.569$$

4th year's insurance to provide for death between 38 and 39

$$\frac{1842}{979217} \times 1{,}000 \times .88849 = 1.671$$

5th year's insurance to provide for death between 39 and 40

$$\frac{2033}{979217} \times 1{,}000 \times .86261 = 1.791$$

6th year's insurance to provide for death between 40 and 41

$$\frac{2242}{979217} \times 1{,}000 \times .83748 = 1.917$$

7th year's insurance to provide for death between 41 and 42

$$\frac{2479}{979217} \times 1{,}000 \times .81309 = 2.058$$

8th year's insurance to provide for death between 42 and 43

$$\frac{2743}{979217} \times 1{,}000 \times .78941 = 2.211$$

9th year's insurance to provide for death between 43 and 44

$$\frac{3044}{979217} \times 1{,}000 \times .76642 = 2.382$$

10th year's insurance to provide for death between 44 and 45

$$\frac{3370}{979217} \times 1{,}000 \times .74409 = 2.561$$

Total = Rs. 19.036

This is net single premium, that is, total cost of 10 year's assurance

Rs. 19.036 is the single premium for 10 year's Term Assurance of Rs. 1,000/-

8. Pure Endowment Premium (PE): Under a pure endowment assurance, payment of the sum assured is made only to those who survive to the end of the term selected. The single premium for 10 years' Pure Endowment Assurance can be calculated as follows:

Out of 9,79,217 persons opting for this scheme at age 35, 9,56,840 survive upto age 45, who will have to be paid Rs. 1,000/- each. The chance of survival to age 45 is 9,56,840/979257. The cost of insurance is therefore 9,56,840/9,79,257 × 1000, which is the amount we should have at the end of 10 years. The present value today of this amount at 3% compound interest is 9,56,840/9,79,217 × 1000 × .74409 = 727.09. This is the single premium for pure endowment which is the product of (1) the chance of survival to the end of the period (2) sum assured and (3) discounting factor for compound interest for a period of ten years.

When we add these two premiums Rs. 19.06 and Rs. 727.09, we get a single premium for an endowment assurance of Rs. 1,000/- for a period of ten years.

If 6% compound interest rate is assumed, these two premiums will work out to Rs. 16.05 and Rs. 545.63, generating single premium for endowment assurance for 10 years of Rs. 561.88. If we assume 0% interest, obviously these rates amount to Rs. 22.15 and Rs. 977.15 totalling Rs. 1,000.

9. Annual Premium for 10-years Endowment: The single premium above represents cost of insurance. But people prefer premium payments on yearly, half yearly, quarterly or monthly basis because the cost of instalment premium would be low and it is more convenient to pay such amounts. While calculating annual premium, we have to take into account the probability of receiving each premium. First premium will be paid by everyone of 979217. But for second premium, only 977807 persons will be living. Hence, the chance of receiving first premium $\frac{979217}{979217}$, second premium $\frac{977807}{979217}$ and so on until 10th premium which will be paid by 960210 persons.

Hence the probability of receiving 10th premium is $\frac{960250}{979217}$.

Each of these ten premiums are to be discounted at 3% compounding interest. Thus, the ten values that would be obtained by multiplying probability of receiving each premium and the relevant compound interest factors would be respectively.

$1 \times 1, \frac{977807}{979217} \times .97087, \frac{976272}{979217} \times .94260 \frac{974593}{979217} \times .91514$

$\frac{972751}{979217} \times .88849, \frac{970718}{979217} \times 86261, \frac{968476}{979217} \times .83748$

$\frac{965997}{979217} \times .81309, \frac{963254}{979217} \times .78941, \frac{960210}{979217} \times .76642$

Solving and adding we get ten figures Re. 1.00, Rs. 969, Rs. .940, Rs. .911, Rs. .883, Rs. .828, Rs. .802 Rs. .777, Rs. .752 = Rs. 8.751, which the present value of 10 Annual premiums of Re. 1/-. This amount of premium can be regarded as a Life Annuity due for a person aged 35 years. *For arriving at the annual premium payable, we divide single premium already calculated by this present value of annual premiums.* Therefore,

$$\text{Annual Premium} = \frac{746.13}{8.717} = \text{Rs. } 85.50,$$ which is the level annual premium for 10 years endowment assurance. At 6% the annual premium will be Rs. 72.54. At 0% interest,

the annual premium is $\frac{1000}{9.915}$ = Rs. 100.86.

This is called pure or net premium which takes into account the mortality and interest factors. If we make allowance for expenses and other contingencies such as bonus under with profit policy and fluctuations such as inflation etc., we get Office Premium and Tabular Premium respectively. Preparation of these premium rates is a highly mathematical exercise. The Branch of mathematics which deals with this aspect is called Actuarial Science and the person who is well versed in this is called an Actuary, who is a Fellow of the Institute of Actuaries, London, or of Indian Institute of Actuaries.

10. Tabular Premium: The Agent quotes Tabular Premium to his prospect. Insurance companies usually grant rebate for mode of payment — yearly or half yearly and rebates for large sum assured. Practice of Life Insurance Corporation of India is to allow 3% and 1.5% of the tabular premium as the rebate for yearly and half yearly premiums under most of its premiums. For large sum assured the rebate would be Re. 1/- per thousand sum assured if the sum assured is Rs. 25,000 or above and Rs. 2/- per thousand sum assured, if it is Rs. 50,000 and above. Each company will have its own method and scale of granting these rebates.

Let us now study a specimen premium calculation on the basis of above assumptions.

Data: A person aged 35 insures for Re. 1,00,000 under an Endowment with profit plan for 25 years. He needs Double Accident Benefit, for which he has to pay yearly tabular premium of Rs. 42.75 per thousand sum assured.

Basic tabular premium	Rs. 42.75
Less yearly mode rebate @ 3%	- 1.28
Balance =	41.47
Less Rebate for sum assured	- 2.00
Balance =	39.47
Yearly premium for Rs. 1,00,000	Rs. 3,947
Add Rs. 100/- for double accident premium	Rs. 100
Yearly Instalment Premium	Rs. 4,047

Every Insurer will have its own rules concerning minimum and maximum sum assured, premium, age at entry, age at maturity and term of assurance. There would be restrictions as regards mode of payment and rebates for sum assured. Double accident benefit which is available by payment of additional premium may also be restricted upto a certain limit such as Rs. 10 lakhs, Rs. 25 lakhs or Rs. 50 lakhs etc.

Under certain plans, single premium can be paid at the beginning of the contract. Some plans provide for enhancement of premium at the end of 5, 6 or 7 years. Some policies may be accepted with occupational extra or health extra. These will have to be added to the final adjusted tabular premium.

11. Treatment of Substandard Risks: As we have already discussed, the underwriter has to decide whether the particular risk can be accepted at usual/normal rates of premium or whether the same can be accepted with some modified terms. Underwriter has to determine for that the incidence of extra mortality to which the life proposed is exposed. This will have to be done on the basis of proposal forms, medical reports and other special reports. Agent's confidential report also helps in assessing the extra risk involved, if any. *The tabular premium quoted by the insurer applies to those lives who are exposed to normal/basic mortality. These lives are termed as average, normal or sub-standard lives. Those lives which do not conform to the normal mortality* on the basis of insurability factors disclosed in the sources of information, that is, proposal form, medical report etc. are called *under-average, sub-normal or sub-standard lives. These lives are classified according to the incidence of extra mortality involved* and assessment is done for the probable extra mortality displayed by the extent of physical, occupational and moral hazards involved.

12. Underwriting Methods: The Judgement method consists of deciding on the basis of reports of medical referee, actuary and others. The decision is subjective and can be arrived at only by skilled personnel. Risk appraisal being a technical job, probably, needs centralised set-up. If the business volume is fairly large, the judgement method may not be ideal. Moreover, for a decentralised system working as in LICI, this method may not serve the purpose. Yet in high sum assured proposals or in proposals with special adverse features, this scheme would be very useful and is still practised in respect of some select proposals.

Numerical Method of Rating

This is a systematic method of measuring each of the factors which influence mortality. For every unfavourable factor debit is raised and for favourable factors credit is given. The final total gives the net extra mortality to which a particular life is exposed. The underwriter has to decide terms of acceptance on the basis of final debit.

Let us take a group of 1000 normal lives aged 35. Our experience shows that 12 persons are expected to die during the year. We have another group of 1,000 lives aged 35 suffering from high B.P. and the expected number of deaths during the course of the year is 20. It is thus seen that the high B.P. group is expected to have 8 extra deaths. Expressed as a percentage of the basic mortality, it amounts to 50% extra mortality rate.

The nature of extra risk has also to be taken into account by the underwriter. e.g. impairments like high B.P. or personal history of heart disease result in increasing incidence of extra risk as the age advances. The reasoning holds good for family history of cardiovascular ailments, resulting in early death. On the other hand, extra risk of underweight or personal history of tuberculosis or respiratory diseases goes on diminishing as the age advances. In case of occupational risks, extra risk remains constant by and large. However, there are certain occupations where a health hazard persists even after employment has ceased.

The underwriter has to keep these aspects in mind, before arriving at a decision.

It may be noted that age itself is an instance of increasing extra risk.

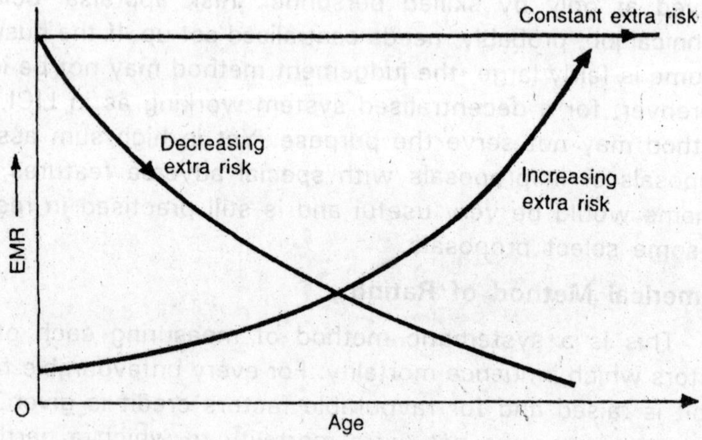

Where more than one impairment is present, the simple rule is to assume that the combined effect of these extra specific mortalities would be equivalent arithmetical addition of these mortality rates. This is known as rule of addition of two or more specific mortalities or Lindquist's Rule. Of course, in appropriate cases, the underwriter is free to modify this rule.

13. Methods of Treating Sub-standard Lives: The terms of the proposal, which are in the nature of an offer can be modified to provide for the extra risk involved. Some of the methods are as under:

Increase in premium is the most common method. One way is to raise up proposer's age by 3 to 5 years. In other words, a 25-year old person would pay premium applicable to a person aged 28 or 30 years. This method cannot be applied if the risk is of decreasing type. This method is not used for one more reason. In the Endowment type of assurance, difference of 3 to 5 years does not make a significant difference in premium rates. Flat extra premium appropriate to extra mortality is usually charged in the majority of proposals which display constant or increasing extra risk. In the decreasing type of risk also, this method can be followed, provided the extra risk does not disappear rapidly in which case the *lien method* has to be followed. If the *extra risk is constant for some period of the policy term,* the extra premium may be charged for a temporary term only. e.g., extra premium for operated hernia would be applicable for a period of two years from the date of such operation. If the decrease in extra risk does not reduce fast but gradually, this method may be followed.

Decrease in Death Benefits

(a) *'Lien' is a contingent debt on the policy. If the life assured dies when the lien is operative, the sum assured will be paid after deducting the amount of lien.* The lien can be constant or decreasing. Constant lien can be imposed in case of certain category of female lives, illiterate lives and possibility of the presence of a moral hazard. Decrease in lien is placed if the risk is of a decreasing type, such as moderate underweight or personal or family history of certain respiratory ailments, if many years have elapsed since the cessation of ailment or cessation of association with such family member. Here the amount of lien/debt goes on reducing every year by a level amount. If a proposal is accepted with a decreasing/ diminishing lien of 500 for 5 years, the sum assured payable in first year of the policy would be Rs. 1,000 – Rs. 500 = Rs. 500, in the second year Rs. 1,000 – Rs. 400 = 600 and so on, so that after the end of the 5th year the policy comes in force for full sum assured. 'Diminishing Lien' as a method is not ideal because it reduces life cover, when it is needed most. Normally, it is allowed if the life assured is young, is moderately underweight and requests for imposition of diminishing lien.

Restrictive Clauses: The extra risk may be of such a nature that so long as it persists it would be difficult to accept it. However, if the extra risk can be excluded the remaining risk can be accepted at normal rates. The usual restrictive exclusions are suicide clause, pregnancy clauses, war and aviation clauses. However, a particular specific element cannot be excluded by such clauses.

Change in the Plan and Period of Assurance: In case of certain increasing types of risks, or a constant heavy risk, a short term endowment may be allowed or a high risk plan such as double or triple term assurance can be changed into single term assurance plan. In case of unsatisfactory family history, displaying early deaths of family members, term may be reduced so that policy does not mature beyond particular age, say 55 or 60. In case of occupations involving health hazards or in case of heavy overweight or other cardiovascular ailments, maturity age may be brought down.

The aforesaid methods may be combined in respect of one single policy displaying heavy risk.

Postponement: *Consideration of the proposal may be deferred or postponed on account of present extra hazard which may disappear after a certain time, when the immediate risk would be over.* This method is followed in cases of heavy overweights or underweights, or recent convalescence after long or serious illness or operation or injuries. If the proposer has a previous policy and on comparison with previous measurement a sudden heavy loss or increase in weight is observed, consideration of proposal may be postponed.

Declinature: In extreme cases, where medical examination discloses that the proposer cannot be covered even by charging extra premium or enough mortality experience is not available or EMR is very high, the underwriter may decline the proposal.

14. Hazard is any factor that adds to the risk. Hazard (Peril in General Insurance) causes the loss to take place. Thus hazard (peril) is the cause, loss is the effect. In popular parlance loss is equated with claim, though it may not be so. Loss may take place, yet a claim may not be payable. Because claim is payable or not payable in accordance with policy conditions. If the cause of the loss, that is the peril, is an uninsured or excluded one, the claim may not be payable, e.g., accidental death or disability taking place as a result of mountaineering etc. Suicide is an excluded peril for a period of one year from the date of F.P.R. It is a permanent exclusion for Double Accident Benefit.

Hazards are of Three Types

(1) ***Physical Hazard:*** This is specific to age, sex, build (height, weight, chest, abdomen measurements) blood pressure, pulse rate, specific gravity of urine — i.e., personal condition, which will also include defects in vision, hearing, walking etc. any other physical defect, personal history of illnesses, injuries, operations etc. Family history relating to early deaths or long survival of family members, previous insurance history also are of material importance. *Failure to disclose these is a material non-disclosure.*

(2) ***Occupational Hazard:*** If the occupation is hazardous, extra premium has to be charged depending on the extent of hazard involved. Certain occupational risks are not covered by extra premium, but the extra risk involved is excluded by applying exclusion clauses. Sometimes, both the methods may be employed. A few occupational risks are declined. e.g. jockeys, riding boys (horse racing) explorers, steeple Jack.

(3) ***Moral Hazard:*** If insurance is taken without genuine need for the same, moral hazard may be present. Over insurance (without the capacity to pay) also suggests a moral hazard. It involves good faith, personal reputation, character, ethics, speculation, etc. of the proposer. If the behaviour of the proposer is not in conformity with the accepted behavioural norms, moral hazard should be suspected. If a moral hazard is present, the proposal has to be dropped or rejected. Extra mortality resulting from moral hazards cannot be measured. The possibility of non-disclosure of material facts cannot be ruled out. Speculative purpose can be suspected. No amount of premium can be adequate to meet a moral hazard.

The common situations that may give rise to moral hazard are:

(1) Absence of insurable interest.

(2) Insurance not supported by income.

(3) Heavy insurance at advanced age.

(4) Insurance in quick succession.

(5) Insuring at a place other than normal residence.

(6) Suppression of previous insurance history.

(7) Nominating a stranger.

(8) Assignment without natural love and affection and without or with inadequate consideration.

(9) Address c/o Agent. In fact address c/o someone else should be enquired into.

15. Methods of Calculating Economic Risk in Life Insurance Proposal: Purpose of life insurance as a risk cover, as a savings medium and as an investment tool is easily understood. But the economic purpose of life insurance is often overlooked. Human life as an income-generating asset for his family members is not presented in proper focus. For understanding the security aspect of life insurance, one has to visualise a human life, as one capable of providing a continuous income to his dependants.

It is true no value can be put on human life. In fact, every person has an unlimited insurable interest in his own life. If does not mean that one can take out life insurance for any amount. So this *principle of insurable interest is tempered by two parameters. viz., capacity to pay and need for insurance.* Yet these three principles do not give any idea as to how much life insurance one needs.

It was Prof. Hubner who related life insurance to the economic activity of man, through his famous Human life Value concept. For this purpose human life as an the economic asset is likened to physical asset. The HLV concept is developed as the economic basis of life insurance. It is to be given the same economic treatment for preservation and capitalisation of physical asset. It provides full indemnity if adequate insurance is taken and through savings builds up capital or asset, so that economic value of the human asset which reduces to zero at old age is replaced by life insurance.

Measurement of human life value is possible with the help of compound interest functions. There are five steps in this procedure.

(1) Estimate the individual's average annual earnings from personal efforts over the remaining years of productive life (E).

(2) Deduct income tax, life insurance premiums and cost of self maintenance (M).

(3) Fix number of years between the individual's present age and expected age of retirement (N).

(4) Select a reasonable rate of interest at which future earnings are to be discounted.

(5) Deduct (2) from (1). Multiply by the present value of Re.1/- per annum for the period determined as in (3), discount at a given rate in (4)

$$HLV = (E - M) \times a_N$$

It should be appreciated that economic value of a producer diminishes with passage of time, because the remaining period of productivity becomes shorter. The unrealised earnings go down, as his potential income is converted into actual income, his economic value diminishes.

Let us take an individual aged 30 years with yearly income of Rs. 1,00,000/- with future expected working life span of 30 years. His expenses are as follows:

LI premium	Rs. 10,000
Income Tax	Rs. 7,000
Personal Expenditure	Rs. 18,000
Income devoted to self	Rs. 25,000
Total	Rs. 60,000

Hence expected income for the family for the remaining 30 years = Rs. 40,000 × 30

= Rs. 12,00,000

But the present value of these 30 payments of Rs. 40,000 discounted today at a reasonable rate of interest, say 9%, can be worked out. Present value interest factor for an annuity of Re.1/- for a period of 30 years @ 9% is given by the formula

$$\frac{1-\frac{1}{(1+i)^n}}{i}$$

where i = 9 & n = 30. The ready reckoner gives this as 10.274.

Therefore, 40,000 × 10.274 = 4,10,960. So this should be the ideal amount for which he should be insured. Since he is paying LIP of Rs. 10,000, he should already be having life insurance of about Rs. 2,00,000. Hence, he has to take additional insurance of Rs. 2,00,000/-.

One has also to take into account his present assets, their nature and his future plans for acquiring these assets. Thus Human Life Value approach should be accompanied by a detailed Capital Needs Analysis. Thus the HLV approach provides a scientific basis for selling/marketing life insurance. The present trend in Western countries is to combine this with traditional needs analysis. The needs approach takes into account the present pressing needs of the person. Hence, his full purchasing potential may not be exploited. However, 'needs approach' is considered as more practical. These needs are classified as —

(1) Clean up fund (last sickness, burial/funeral expenses, outstanding loans, inheritance costs etc.

(2) Readjustment income-in standard of living etc.

(3) Life income for the spouse.

(4) Special needs of the family.

(5) Retirement needs.

These needs would differ according to the individual status of the person and the stage of the life cycle in which he is at present i.e. single with dependent parents, recently married and dependent parents, married with children, family member with physical/mental disability, person with heavy mortgage loan etc.

16. Five-Needs Analysis: A.H. Maslow, psychologist, developed 5-level needs analysis, based on concept of need priority. These are projected on a trapezium.

The needs at two lower levels are physiological and dominate human priorities. If these are well-satisfied, persons move upto the higher order needs. Life insurance can be helpful in satisfying these needs. The marketing personnel has to identify these needs and sell an appropriate policy to the prospect.

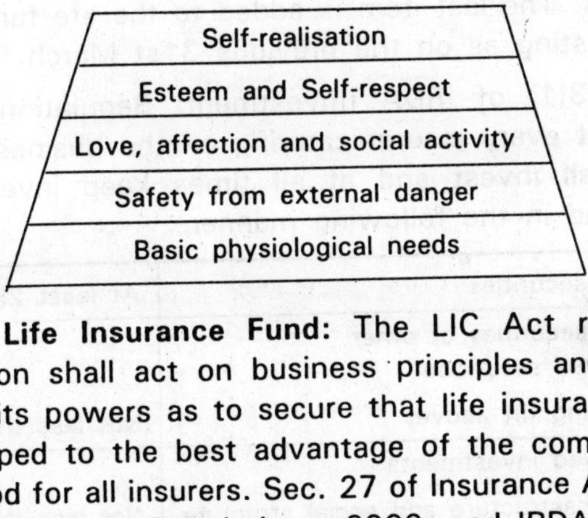

17. Life Insurance Fund: The LIC Act requires that Corporation shall act on business principles and it shall so exercise its powers as to secure that life insurance business is developed to the best advantage of the community. This holds good for all insurers. Sec. 27 of Insurance Act read with IRDA (Investment) Regulations, 2000, and IRDA (Preparation of Financial statements and Auditor's Report of Insurance Companies) Regulations, 2000, amply speak for themselves. For a life insurance fund, security of the capital is very important. Life insurer is a trustee of policyholder's money. Life insurance contracts are long-term contracts. Hence, *the life insurer must have* with it, at any point of time, *sufficient*

funds to meet contractual liabilities. *Earning the highest possible interest, subject to safety of capitals* is the second basic requirement of investment of Life Insurance Fund.

The two principal sources of income of a life insurance company are *premiums and interest earned on investments.* (A). The major expenses, apart from the claim liabilities, are agent's commission and commission related expenses, medical fees, printing and stationery, publicity and advertisement costs, administrative costs, including staff salaries. *The excess of income over expenditure would disclose surplus (and not profit).* The expenditure is grouped under following heads. (A) Commission and operating expenses related to insurance business, including depreciation (B) Benefits paid, interim bonuses paid, (C) change in valuation of liabilities and reinsurance ceded and accepted

Surplus/Deficit (D) = (A) – (B) – (C)

This is to be appropriated to shareholder's account, transfer to other reserves and transfer to funds for future appropriations. The last item is added to the life fund which is already existing as on the previous 31st March.

Section 3(1) of IRDA (Investment) Regulations, 2000 stipulates that every insurer carrying on the business of life insurance shall invest and at all times keep invested his controlled fund in the following manner.

(i) Govt. securities	At least 25%
(ii) Govt. securities or other approved securities (including (i)(above)	Not less than 50%
(iii) Approved investments (a) Infrastructure and social structure	Not less than 15%
(b) others governed by exposure/prudential norms	Not exceeding 20%
(iv) other to be governed by exposure/prudential norms	Not exceeding 15%

However, for pension and general Annuity business these percentages are (i) 20% (ii) 40% (iii) 60%.

The controlled fund thus would directly go up by the amount of interest earned. However, accretion to fund depends upon generation of surplus, a major portion of which is added to the existing life fund. This would arise as a result of three surpluses:

(i) Mortality surplus arises if actual mortality experience is favourable/better than one assumed in premium calculation. This surplus would be moderated/tempered/ affected by the mortality assumptions made in the valuation process. If a lower proportion of policyholders die than assumed, then there would be mortality surplus.

(ii) If the actual interest earned is more than the one provided in the premium table, there would be interest surplus.

(iii) While fixing the office premium, the actuary assumes a certain percentage of premium (usually 1/8% to 1%) as policyholder's share of expenses . If the insurer can keep down his actual expenses within this assumed limit, there would be expense surplus.

If the experience becomes or proves to be unsatisfactory, there would be deficit instead of surplus. *Thus, generation of surplus reflects upon quality of underwritng, investments and administration.*

18. Valuation: Under Sec. 13 of the Insurance Act, every insurer carrying on life insurance business must cause an investigation to be made by an actuary into the financial condition of the life insurance business carried by it every year. IRDA (Assets, Liabilities and Solvency Margin of Insurers) Regulations, 2000, provide detailed guidelines about valuation procedure. Every insurer has to prepare a statement of the value of assets (Reg. 3), a statement of the amount of liabilities (Reg. 4) and a statement of solvency margin (Reg. 5) in a prescribed format. Valuation has to be done by the prospective method. (Ref. Reg. 3(4)(v) of IRDA (Acturial Report) Regulations 2000).

IRDA (Assets, Solvency) Regulations 2000 Reg. (6) terms this as Gross Premium Method. In this method specific provision for future bonuses is not made but mortality, interest and expense rate assumed will take care of this. If the variation discloses surplus, 90% of this surplus is allocated to the policyholders and 10% will be available for allocation to shareholders, who however can relinquish the same. As far as LICI is concerned, Sec. 26 of LIC Act 1956 stipulates that acturial valuation shall be done every two years (every year for all Insurers) from 1986 onwards by LIC and as per amended Section 13 of Insurance Act, 1938 from 2000 onwards. If the surplus is disclosed, Section 28 of LIC Act stipulates at least 95 per cent should be allocated to the with-profit policyholders, and the remainder shall be paid to the Central Government or utilised for such purposes as Central Government may direct. LICI follows Gross Premium Method of valuation. For other Insurers IRDA's Guidelines apply.

19. Distribution of Bonus: Under the *Simple Reversionary Method*, the bonus declared attaches to the policy and becomes a part of the sum assured. For example, if Endowment Bonus of Rs. 70/- is declared per thousand sum assured, the liability of the insurer stands increased by Rs. 70/- and the amount payable on maturity or death if earlier would be Rs. 1,070/- If the policy is for 20 years, 20 bonuses in all, would be added to the sum assured and would be payable alongwith it. In the *Compound Reversionary System*, the bonus declared in one year ranks and is eligible for bonus declared in the next and subsequent years. e.g. in the aforestated example, if next year's bonus rate is again @ Rs. 70/- per thousand sum assured, actual amount of allocated bonus would be on S.A. of Rs. 1,070/- and not Rs. 1,000. Hence, 2nd years' effective bonus would be 70 + 4.90 = Rs. 74.90. If the bonus rate remains the same in the third year also, effective bonus would be calculated on Rs. 70 + Rs. 74.90 = Rs. 144.90. So the declared rate of Rs. 70/- would actually work out to Rs. 80.14. Thus every year, effective accrued bonus will increase at a very rapid rate. Obviously the policyholder will have to pay higher premium rate if he opts for this scheme.

Cash Bonus or Encashment Bonus: Both the bonuses can be encashed. The cash value of bonus, which is due for payment after many years, would be a small amount. But, it works as a selling point. The cash value is applied to reduce next year's premium. In effect therefore, the policyholder needs to pay full premium only in the first one or two years. Thereafter, he will always be paying less amount provided the company keeps on declaring bonus. LICI does not practise this method. It allows encashment of bonus only if the entire policy contract is surrendered.

Contributory Bonus: Under this method, every policyholder gets bonus in the same proportion which his policy reserve bears to the total reserve. Tontine bonus is paid only to those who survive. Since the system is inequitable, it is not in vogue.

Terminal Bonus/Final Additional Bonus is paid to those policies which are in force for at least 15 years at the time of claim either by maturity or death. This bonus can be said to be an incentive to super-standard policyholders.

Interim Bonus: Sec. 112 of the Insurance Act permits the insurer to declare interim bonus at the rate of bonus declared at previous valuation in respect of those policies which become claim either by maturity or by death during Intervaluation Period.

SELF-STUDY QUESTIONS

1. What do you understand by 'Mortality'? Write a brief note on the subject.
2. Explain the concept of Risk Premium.
3. Describe the three components of premium.
4. What is underwriting? Explain how it operates.
5. Explain how expenses are analysed.
6. What are the various methods of treating sub-standard lives? Discuss these briefly.
7. What is moral hazard? How does an underwriter deal with it.
8. Explain in detail the HLV concept of Prof. Hubner.
9. Write a short note on Needs Analysis?
10. Generation of surplus reflects upon the quality of underwriting, investment and administration. Discuss.
11. Explain the principle behind granting of terminal bonus.
12. What are the legal bases for declaration of bonus and investment of life insurance funds.

13. Calculate Instalment Premium on the basis of following data.

Age yrs.	Plan-Term yrs.	Sum Assured Rs.	Tabular Yly/ Premium per thousand S.A. Rs.	Mode of Payment	How accepted
(a) 26	End-25	50,000	56.00	Qtrly	With DAB
(b) 35	End-20	1,00,000	68.00	Yly.	With DAB + Health extra of Rs. 2.50%
(c) 42	Double cover-15	2,00,000	83.50	Yly.	With DAB
(d) 28	Money Back-20	25,000	59.25	Hly.	With occupational extra Rs. 2% + DAB
(e) 24	Term Assurance-10	5,00,000	10.10/-	Yly.	—

Assume DAB @ Re. 1/- per thousand. S.A.
Mode Rebates Yly - 3% of the Tabular Premium. Hly 1.5% of T.P. S.A. Rebate - 25,000 - 49,000 - Re. 1/- per thousand over Rs. 50,000/- Rs. 2/- per thousand.

14. Write short notes on
  (a) Mortality Table (b) Valuation Process
  (c) Compound Reversionary Bonus (d) Tabular Premium
  (e) Life Fund.

KEY WORDS/PHRASES TO REMEMBER

Law of Large Numbers

Mortality

Risk-Net-Office-Tabular Premium

Rebates for mode — SA.

Substandard Life

Numerical Method

Physical — Occupational — Moral Hazards

Human Life Value Approach

Needs Approach

Valuation — Gross Premium Prospective methods of Bonus Computation.

❑❑❑

4

Life Insurance — Policies

Objectives

To provide an understanding about various life insurance products and various legal provisions affecting life insurance contract.

Lesson Objectives

To enable the students to understand:

(1) Application of insurance policies in different situations.

(2) Composition of various plans.

(3) Significance of annuities in changed demographic scenario.

(4) Important legal provisions.

(5) Important judicial pronouncements.

Life Insurance is a peculiar product. An Insurance product is intangible as against commercial products which are tangible. Products which we see, feel and we can have physical possession and enjoyment of are tangible products. A product, whose presence is felt through its servicing aspect is called an intangible product. Life insurance is an intangible product and populerly goes by the name Insurance Policy. Policy describes the selected plan. Thus, we can say that the various plans are really products through which an Insurance company sells its ideas. The company must ensure the quality of the product, since what is sold is merely a promise — though a contractual promise. The presence of this product is felt when a promise is replaced by 'money' — by way of settlement of claims — whether on maturity or on death. With this money the daily living of the insured person or his dependents will be sustained.

A Life Insurance product continues to exist over a long period of time. And for keeping the contract in force, the insured person has to go on paying the purchase price — called premium, throughout the term of the policy, so that benefits already secured are not lost. Life Insurance is thus a product with a difference.

One more feature of this product is that *it is seldom bought but sold.* The purchaser needs to be motivated to buy. Prompt and efficient servicing acts as a motivating force. The *consumption of this product extends over a long time.* The agent has to take into account needs of the purchaser and suggest to him the type of policy he should purchase. His principal, that is, the insurance company, relies on the statements made by the purchaser, who has to fill-up and sign a written proposal form, which becomes the basis of he contract. Hence, *Life Insurance products are sold as a part of the contract which is subject to the principle of utmost good faith (Uberimae Fides).*

Even as a service-oriented product, it offers a different kind of service from other types of services such as water supply, electricity, gas supply, transport service or even from banking service, for that matter.

Product pricing becomes a highly technical — mathematical job in the pricing process of life insurance products. The determination of premium or price for the insurance product involves a lot of statistical analysis and forecasting of future probabilities of dying and survival of specific segments of the population. i.e., of policyholders. *The three basic components of this cost price are mortality, interest and expenses.* Interestingly, the insurer has little control over the first two factors. The third component can be checked to some extent but not controlled fully, because many causes of increase in expenses lie beyond the control of the insurer. Though mortality rates of insured population are improving, generally, insurer has no control over it. Interest rates in this country are under state-review and control. Hence, when the interest rates are modified by the government agency, the insurer has to take immediate steps to reduce the impact of future probable losses on account of these huge important underlying components of a life insurance premium. Therefore during the last three years, when interest rates have steadily been coming down, the insurance companies are required to terminate old plans and bring in a new one with lower rates of interest. Life Insurance Corporation of India is performing this exercise in respect of certain plans. Some private insurers have also followed this practice in respect of a few of their plans.

These plans are really the products through which the company sells, its idea of insurance. The company has to *maintain quality of the product, backed by unmatched service.* These plans should *satisfy the needs of the consumer — economic and financial needs.* Returns combined with cheap death cover should be backed by effective, prompt and proper service.

Life insurance products are combinations of two basic insurance plans — Term Assurance and Pure Endowment.

Term Assurance

As its name indicates, it is an assurance for a term. If the insured person dies during the selected term, insurer pays the sum assured. If the insured person survives the term, the premium paid and adjusted by the insurer is not refunded. In other words, *nothing is payable as survival benefit under a term assurance plan.*

Modern life insurance originated in 17th century England in the form of Term Assurance for one year (OYTA). However, this scheme was found to be inadequate as a long-term plan of insurance. The basic drawback of this plan was that renewal every year was not compulsory. Hence, the persons especially healthy persons, would drop out of the scheme, since they were reasonably sure that the probability of their dying in the next year was negligible. Thus, only those persons who were not so healthy, or who were not sure whether they would survive at the end of the next year continued with the scheme. The result was that *these schemes were saddled with sub-standard lives, resulting in adverse claims experience. In due course, annual level premium plan was evolved.* The basic principle however remained the same. i.e. sum assured became payable only on the death of the life assured.

Term Insurances are usually for a term of 5-years and over. However, One Year's Term Assurance (OYTA) is granted under group insurance schemes, where premium is reviewed every year and there are no maturity benefits as such under these policies. Under the individual type of policies, *Level-Premium Term Assurance is being sold by all life insurers throughout the world.* However, since term assurance has no maturity benefit, it is not quite popular in our country. However, in European countries, in U.S.A. and Canada, Term Assurances are quite popular.

Common characteristics of any term assurance plan are: cheap provision for dependents and a pure risk cover without any return on investment. Term Assurance offers life insurance cover for a specific number of years, at the least cost with no survival benefits. It is life insurance in the simplest form, it covers the risk of dying too early. If the price becomes the dominant consideration, Term Assurance is the cheapest form of assurance.

Term policies are available for a tenure between five and twenty-five years The term of the policy should be retirement specific, that is it should not exceed the remaining years of active working life. Even if one is adequately insured, there may be circumstances in which it would be prudent to go in for additional term insurance for short duration. This may be necessary if you are running extra financial risk for a few years. e.g. repayment of housing loan or car loan. To popularise term plans insurers have a term assurance with return of premium on maturity. Under one policy of LIC even after ROP, a free term cover for reduced sum continued for further ten years (Bima Kiran).

A Comparative Chart of Term Assurance Premiums

Age	*LIC*	*ICICI Pru.*	*HDFC Std.*	*Birla Sun Life*
25	1601	2327	2620	2890
30	2037	2504	2820	2950
35	2910	2925	3050	3310
40	4462	3601	3790	4310
45	7227	5336	5520	5990

(Yearly Premium for 10-year policy for sum assured of Rs. 10 lakhs.)

These Term Assurances are available under Single Premium Basis also.

Since the premiums are very low, these plans are 'without profit', i.e. these policies are not entitled to any bonus declared by the company as a result of annual valuation.

Two year's Temporary Term Assurance comes in handy when you need a risk cover for a short period of less than two years. These policies may be available for a duration of 6 months, 1 year 6 months and 2 years. The premium is to be paid once only. For a person aged 35 years the one-time premium is Rs. 7/- per thousand sum assured. These policies are not entitled to surrender value and to loan, thereunder. The premium would be as low as Rs. 3.40 at age 18 for 6 months assurance while maximum premium payable is Rs. 42.85 at age 60 for 2-year's assurance. Satisfactory proof of age must be produced. The cost of medical examination is borne by the life assured.

Term Assurance need not be constant all along. If the prospect's need goes on reducing every year a Reducing or Decreasing Term Assurance can be arranged. This plan is designed to meet the requirements of loanees of Housing or car-finance, who are repaying the loan every month. The creditor company quotes a uniform repayment amount cover Equated Monetary Instalment (EMI). The matching requirement is that of a Decreasing Term Assurance. The policy term matches with the loan repayment term. A schedule showing amount of loan outstanding at the beginning of each year is shown on the policy document on the basis of predetermined interest. The insurer will pay the liability as shown in the policy document irrespective of actual loan repayments. The loan has to be liquidated before the age of 65. Premium paying term is usually limited to two thirds of the period of repayment of loan. There is no surrender value available under this policy.

Convertible Term Assurance

This is a unique policy for youngsters, who need insurance but would not like to put more money into Life Insurance. Premiums are payable for 5 or 6 or 7 years. These policies are not normally permitted beyond the age of 50 or 55. At the end of the stipulated period, the life assured has an option to convert the policy into limited payment whole life or endowment, when he will have to pay enhanced premium thereafter.

Increasing Term Assurance is one where sum assured at risk increases at periodic intervals. A typical Moneyback or Cash cover policy provides the example. Under this policy, a certain predetermined percentage of the basic sum assured is paid out, say every 5 years. If the policy is for a 25 years term, the life assured will be getting 4-instalments during the terms of the policy at the end of the 5th, 10th, 15th and 20th year respectively at 15% each. On maturity he will get the balance of 40% of the sum assured with bonuses on full sum assured. However, on death at anytime during the currency of the policy, provided the policy is in force, full sum assured becomes payable without deducting the amounts already paid to him. In effect, this amounts to increasing term assurance, since the total payout under the policy, in case of a death claim, would be 100%, 115%, 130%, 145% and 160% of the basic sum assured, if the death takes place during 0-5 years, 5-10 years, 10-15 years, 15-20 or 20-25 years respectively. Thus, the sum at risk goes on increasing periodically in such assurances.

Floating Term Assurance

Under this policy, a free term assurance is available for a period of three years provided at least two years' premiums have been received. The FTA operates from the third year onwards. Even if the life assured fails to pay premium for a continuous period of 3 years, *he is eligible for a Term Assurance equal to the basic sum assured.* It means that if the life assured dies at any time during this 3 years' period, full sum assured is payable, subject to recovery of unpaid premiums with interest thereon. The peculiarity of this plan is that this concession is available throughout the term of the policy. If the policyholder is alive at the end of this three year period, the policy will lapse or become paid-up, as the case may be. This policy can be revived subject to payment of arrears of premium with interest at any time during the term of the policy, subject to rules of the Company in this behalf.

Whole Life Assurances

When the term of insurance extends to cover whole life i.e. until death of the life assured, it is known as whole life assurance. *Theoretically, the premiums under the policy must be paid until death.* The sum assured becomes payable only after the death. Obviously this policy is not useful, *since the premiums are payable for a very long period and only death-risk is covered and premiums are low. In practice however, insurers agree to pay the sum assured with accrued bonuses, if any, on life assured's completion of 100 years.* It is interesting to know the historical background of this practice. In 1957, the Life Insurance Corporation decided to waive premiums under whole life policies after completion of 80 years of age 35 years premium paying period, whichever is later, sum assured being payable on death. Maharshi Dhondo Keshav Karve, a social reformer in the field of widows' education was born on 18th April 1858. His birth centenary was celebrated on 18th April 1958. Maharshi Karve had purchased two whole life insurance policies — one for Rs. 3,000 and the other for Rs. 5,000 in 1883. According to the policy condition, the sum assured with bonuses would have been payable only on his death. He lived for 105 years. The premiums under this policy had already been waived. The LIC decided to settle these two claims on his completion of 100 years of his age. In fact, a policy decision was taken accordingly. Dr. Moropant V. Joshi was another beneficiary of this decision. The new private insurers who have entered the Indian Market recently have decided to follow this practice of settling whole life policy claims on completion by life assured of 100 years of age. LICI now pays sum assured on completion of 80 years of life assured's age.

Though the premiums are to be paid until the death of the life assured, in practice, insurers allow premium payment to be continued for 80 years of age or 35 years term whichever is later. Premiums are low. e.g. a person aged 30 years would pay about Rs. 25/- per year for a sum assured of Rs. 1,000/-. Without profits policy payments are to be made for 25 years term or upto 70 years of age, whichever is later.

The alternative is also available in the form of the whole life limited payment plan. The life assured pays the premiums during his ordinary productive years, say upto the age of 60 or 70. The peculiarity of this policy is that even after premium payment has ceased, the policy continues to participate in bonus thereafter till life assured's death. Annual premium for a without profit and with profit is around Rs. 15/- and Rs. 32/- only. These policies are available on single premium basis also. LIC and most of the private insurers offer whole life plans. Some companies split the premium into 2 parts, pure cover (term cover) and savings element. The savings element itself is available under 3 options — Protector (low risk), Builder (medium risk) or Enhancer (high risk). Bonus rates under Whole Life policies are higher than under Endowment Assurance Policies. Recently, LICI has discontinued its without profits plan.

Convertible Whole Life Assurance

This is similar to convertible term assurance described above, the difference being that at the end of the initial 5 years, if the life assured does not exercise the option of conversion into endowment plan, it automatically converts into a whole life policy without profits, with premiums ceasing at age 70. If the option is exercised for a with-profit plan, policy starts participating in profits from the date of the conversion.

Combination Plans

Whole Life cum Endowment Plan: Under this plan, Life assured is covered for a whole life assurance, which gives him death risk cover alongwith accrued bonus upto that date and the policy ceases. If the life assured survives the selected term, he gets the endowment sum assured with accrued bonuses. The whole life assurance for the basic sum assured continues, which becomes payable on death anytime after the completion of the premium paying term. Thus, this plan is a combination of endowment assurance for a selected term and fully-paid up free whole life assurance thereafter. LIC's Jeevan Anand Policy gives these benefits.

Endowment Plans: These are a combination of Term Assurance (TA) and Pure Endowment (PE). These are by far the most popular plans of life insurance. Almost 95% of LIC's policies are of the endowment type. These include traditional Endowment (35%) Money Back policies (35%), Joint Life Endowment and other special Endowment policies.

Under the traditional endowment plan, the life assured is covered for a specified term, not going beyond the age of 70 or 75. If the life assured survives the term, full sum assured, together with due bonuses, if it is a with profit policy, becomes payable and the contract comes to an end. In case of death during this term, sum assured, with due bonuses upto death becomes payable.

The advantage of this plan is that the life assured can make provision for his dependents as also for his old age. Everyone would like to enjoy the fruits of his savings. This also becomes an additional favourable objective under this plan.

The Investment-minded person however, is not quite comfortable with this plan. He would like to have returns from this policy much earlier. He also takes into account the *inflation, which has an eroding effect.* To meet the needs of such policyholders, insurers devise Money Back or Cash Cover policies. These come in various terms from 15 to 25 years. A part of the sum assured is returned periodically. On completion of the selected term only the balance of the sum assured, together with accrued bonuses are paid. However, death at any time during the term of the policy provides full sum assured, without deducting the instalments of the sum assured already paid. *Thus, money back policies give a wider cover than under an ordinary endowment policy.* Hence, these policies are becoming more and more popular among the insuring public.

The periodical return of sum insured may be desired for reasons other than investment returns. Under ordinary Endowment Assurance the sum assured becomes payable only once. i.e., on maturity date (if death does not take place prior – to this date). The policyholder (life assured) who has grown older by 25/30 years by the maturity date, has added financial responsibilities of his family. Hence, he would like to have a part of the sum assured just before maturity. This can be done by providing *money-back at the near-end of the policy term.* Sum assured is paid in specified instalments during the last 5 years of the policy, the principle of full death risk cover operates during this term also. (Jeevan Chhaya of LIC). This policy grants an additional sum assured on death during the term and the future premiums are waived. The periodical instalments continue to be paid to the nominees. Thus, this policy is a combination of double cover Endowment Plan (Jeevan Mitra of LIC) plus Money Back Policy.

Double Cover/Triple Cover Endowment

Under this plan, the term assurance cover is twice that of basic assurance. If the life assured dies during the term of the policy, double or triple the sum assured becomes payable. On maturity however, only the single sum assured with accrued bonuses becomes payable. *For a young man, who has just set up his house, this policy is an ideal one. In a single policy he gets double, triple term cover plus guaranteed endowment portion on maturity.* The bonuses however accrue on the basic sum assured only. In case of double accident cover, 4-times the sum assured may be available in case of death due to accident.

Policy for Persons with Reducing Income

Certain persons like Cine artistes, T.V. artistes have a short but very productive working life. After a few years, their income dwindles. A policy for high sum assured in earlier years may be found difficult to maintain because of high premiums. A typical endowment policy, where annual premium payable in the first 5 years gets reduced to 1/3 of the same from 6th year onwards can meet the requirements of such persons. However, unfortunately such policy is not popular with the targeted segment itself. Possibly prestige may be playing its part because purchasing this policy make be taken as admission of the fact that the artiste will not remain popular at the end of 5 years and that his income will go down.

Policy for Persons with Temporary Stoppage of Income

Indian agriculture is subject to the vagaries of the monsoon. If rains fail, crops may be lost. Excessive rains and floods have a similar impact. The insurance policy taken for a large sum assured, when the income was high, may not be sustained due to loss of or fall in income. This situation may continue for 2/3 years. Like trade cycles, agricultural production also runs through period of ups and downs. In order to meet the requirements of this segment, insurer has devised a plan of endowment type where the death risk cover continues even though the premiums are not paid for three years, provided at least two years premiums have been paid. For every premium paid thereafter, the three years free term is extended by the period for which premiums have been paid. In the present day of unemployment or job losses, this policy is really useful. The New Jan Raksha Policy of LIC is gaining in popularity, precisely for this reason.

Joint Life Assurances

Husband and wife have an insurable interest in each other's lives. Hence, a husband can insure his wife's life, the wife her husband's. Husband and wife can take out a joint life assurance policy also. Under this plan, both persons are medically examined. Both the proposals are underwritten separately. In case one life is uninsurable, this policy cannot be offered. The advantage of this policy is that *a single policy covers both husband and wife.* This is an endowment assurance. Hence, sum assured is paid on completion of the term. However, if one life dies during the term, sum assured is paid immediately, but the policy continues for equal amount of sum assured, for the remaining period of the policy, with all future premiums waived. In other words a free paid-up assurance for an equal amount is granted to the surviving spouse. Both lives can be covered for double accident benefit. If the surviving party dies as a result of accident, in the remaining part of that policy year, Double Accident Benefit is paid in respect of that life as well. This is an Endowment policy with profit. Hence, if both the lives survive the term of the policy, basic sum assured with accrued bonuses, thereon would become payable. *This policy is ideally suited for those couples where both husband and wife are working.*

Partnership Insurance

Business partners have got an insurable interest in each other's lives to the extent of capital brought by each one of them. In the absence of insurance provision, the surviving partner will have to pay the deceased partner's share from partnership funds. To that extent profitability of the concern will be affected. *Partnership Insurance is a single policy granted on the lives of two partners.* This is a fixed term endowment policy. If both partners survive the term, endowment sum assured with bonuses is available to the partnership firm. In case of death of either of the partners, sum assured is paid to the surviving partner, alongwith accrued bonuses upto the date of death of the other partner. In view of the peculiar position of the policy a nominee under Sec. 39 of the Insurance Act need not be nominated. Partnership deed alongwith the supplementary deeds, if any, Copies of Income Tax Returns or Assessment orders for past three years should be examined. Capital Account of the partner as also latest audited Profit and Loss account should also be examined.

An authorised executive of the firm can take out a policy on the life of another partner. In such cases it may be possible to offer keyman insurance on joint lives. The premiums paid under the Partnership Insurance are allowed as expenses under Sec. 37(1) of Income Tax Act, 1961. In an individual policy, proposed by a partnership firm, life assured will be the employee.

Keyman Insurance for Companies

Running of a business enterprise successfully depends upon profitable employment of business assets. This is possible only through organisation and management of business processes. This is the work of competent personnel. Every business has one or two *keymen* who possess the necessary managerial skill and experience to make optimum use of the available resources. If such an employee is lost, the concern will experience a severe financial shock.

An employer has an insurable interest in the life of his employees. More so with the keyman whose *contribution in business* is substantial and significant, hence worthy of insurance. For determining the contribution of a particular employee, many factors are to be considered.

(1) Qualifications of the keyman.

(2) Experience in different areas of operation.

(3) Seniority.

(4) Extent of authority in the specific field.

(5) Total emoluments with perks.

(6) Whether some other employee can be a keyman.

Though it is very difficult to put a monetary value on the individual contribution, the gross profits of the company and employee's stock in that can be compared. However, some checkpoints can be observed:

(1) Shareholding in the company should not be over 50%.

(2) Number of shareholders: 5 to 10.

(3) Number of employees: 5 to 10.

Two times the average of 3 years net profit can be granted as life insurance. For larger organisations 3 times of the average can be considered for insurance.

Normal term under this policy is 10 to 15 years. Policy will not be allowed to mature beyond normal superannuation age.

A Board Resolution for granting insurance to a particular person is necessary. Only the authorised person will sign the proposal papers. Articles of Association and Memorandum should be examined. The policy does not cover double accident benefit and nomination is not necessary. The Claim amount is payable to the Employer.

If the assessee firm taking out the insurance policy is able to establish before the Income Tax Officer that the premium paid on such insurance is an expenditure laid out wholly and exclusively for the purpose of business it will be entitled to a deduction under Section 37(1) of the Income Tax Act, 1961. The policy should not be assigned to the keyman and the policy proceeds should be received by the company. In that case policy proceeds are not liable for Income Tax. Otherwise, the policy proceeds shall be treated as perks in the keyman's hands and taxed accordingly. The policy cannot be assigned to any one except the life assured himself. The employer can also surrender this policy, when the keyman leaves the company.

Keyman insurance is a new segment of the life insurance business which is developing very fast. It gives protection against financial loss in the event of keyman's death. It gives substantial income tax benefits to the company. It gives financial stability to the organisation. This policy is accepted as a security by the creditors.

Children's Assurances

Parents have an insurable interest in the lives of their children as children. Hence, insurance companies offer many plans on children's lives. Some common features of these plans can be described as under.

(1) Child being a minor has no legal right to enter into a contract. Hence, a contract is entered into by the parent.

(2) There is a time gap between the date of commencement of the policy and the date of commencement of death risk on the child's life. This would be the policy anniversary on completion of specified age. This is called Deferred Date, the time gap is called Deferment Period. Though the risk may commence before majority, the child can become the owner of the policy when he completes 18 years of age. The policy anniversary following completion of 18 years/21 years is called Vesting Date. If the deferment period is 10 years or more, the

proposer can get a cash option on the deferred date. If the child dies within the deferment period, policy shall stand cancelled and all the premiums paid will be refunded without deduction. If the proposer dies during the deferment period, policy should be continued. Accident/Disability benefit is allowed only after the deferment period is over. There is no nomination in this policy during deferment period. The parent can cover his risk during the deferment period, by payment of an extra premium to secure premium waiver benefit (PWB). If this is done, in case of parent's death during deferment period, future premiums upto deferred date are waived. In one policy issued by LICI on the life of a female child, husband of the girl is also covered 3 months after marriage on or one month after intimation of marriage or attainment of age 20 by the female child, whichever is later.

After the deferred date children's policy can be continued as an endowment plan or money back plan. (Children's Money Back Plan). Additional benefits in the form of quarterly income can also be provided, on payment of additional premium.

Health-oriented Plans

A life insurance company cannot issue a Mediclaim Policy or Health Insurance Policy. However these can be combined with a regular life insurance policy to cover specified sickness called *critical illness cover* or *dreaded diseases cover*. These are basically endowment policies. If the life assured is not afflicted by any one of the specified diseases and in the manner and extent as stipulated in the policy he will be entitled to survival benefit of 2% every 2nd year. As an alternative to getting survival benefits, health-cost-reimbursement can be enhanced. For specified surgical procedures, life assured will get 20% or 50% of sum assured for minor or major surgery. Life Insurance policy is a fixed benefit policy and not a reimbursement policy. Policy is entitled for loyalty and guaranteed additions for every year's premium received. The major surgical procedures relate to nervous system, respiratory system and cardiovascular system. Certain minor surgical procedures relating to respiratory system, digestive system, liver, gall bladder and pancreas, endocrine system etc. can be covered.

Investment-Oriented Plans

In USA and European countries, flexible insurance policies are getting popular. These are tailor-made to suit the needs of individual needs of the client. Insurers cover mortality guarantee. Interest and expense guarantees are passed on to the consumer. Sum assured is kept separate for which mortality charge is made. A major portion of the premium is utilised to create fund units, which will be invested. The investments will be as per the choice of the life assured — in a secured fund, balanced fund or risk fund — in equity, debt or liquid. The charges that would be recovered from the premium would be mortality charge, Accident cover charge, expense charge, Fund management charge and bid/offer spread charge.

A pure investment oriented plan would be a single premium policy for 5 or 10 years. A single premium of Rs. 952 and Rs. 863 would secure sum assured of Rs. 1,000 at the end of 5 years and 10 years respectively. Guaranteed additions and loyalty additions are added to the sum assured. One can have additional Term Assurance (Term Rider) which shall not exceed the basic sum assured. The return on investment, after taking into account guaranteed and loyalty additions, premium rebate under Sec. 88 and no-tax on maturity amount (Sec. 10(10D) is attractive. LICI sold more than 2 lakh policies of this type during 2001-2002. The Taxation provisions of 2003 Union Budget have affected this plan, adversely.

Guarantees, Options and Riders

IRDA (Actuarial Report and Abstract) Regulations 2000 provide definitions of these terms.

Guarantees means the terms in regard to benefits or premiums or charges, which may not be altered during the currency of the policy.

Options means the rights available to a policyholder under a policy.

Riders or Rider Benefits means add-on benefits which are in addition to basic benefits under a policy.

Guarantees

If the policy is in force for full sum assured the sum assured gets enhanced at the specified guaranteed rate at the end of each year. These additions are payable with the original sum assured. Normally without profit policies are allowed this benefit, which becomes a selling point. Whatever maybe the rate of bonus declared under with-profit policies, Guaranteed additions cannot be altered.

Loyalty additions are over and above guaranteed additions. A policy has to be in force for a minimum period of 2 to 3 years. Rates of loyalty additions are much lower than guaranteed additions. The basic premium takes into account these additions.

Options: There are many options available to the policyholder. Apart from choice of Plan-Term-Sum Assured, he has the option of paying premiums on yearly, half-yearly, quarterly or monthly basis. In some of the plans like convertible whole life, the policyholder has an option to change the plan at the end of five years. Under Children's Deferred Assurance, the proposer has the option of covering death risk on his life during deferment period. Additional Term Assurance can be had by the policyholder, if he so chooses. Double accident benefit can be had by payment of additional premium. Claim amount can be retained with the insurer for some time (called settlement option).

Riders or Conditions

IRDA (Protection of Policyholders Interests Regulations) 2002 – Reg. 3(1) provides as follows.

"The allowable rider or riders on the product shall be clearly spelt out with regard to their scope of benefits and in no case the premium relatable to all the riders put together shall exceed 30% of the premium of the main product.

Explanation: The rider or riders attached to a life policy shall bear the nature and character of the main policy *viz.,* participating or non-participating and accordingly the life insurer shall make provisions etc. in his books. Thus, riders are add-on options that help you to enhance your insurance cover, qualitatively and quantitatively. *Riders allow you to customize your policy to match your needs. Riders provide low cost pure risk cover.* The usual riders are *Level-Term Rider*, which gives you the option to increase your risk cover. Critical illness/

dreaded disease rider provides you additional cover against the risk of your contracting a critical illness, major surgical assistance benefit, accident and disability benefit, waiver of future premium rider, guaranteed insurability rider to enable you to purchase additional insurance in future.

Annuities

Section 2(11)(b) of Insurance Act, 1938 states that life insurance business includes the granting of annuities on human life. The two risks which attach to human life are death and long life. Most of the persons appreciate the need to provide for the family in case of a breadwinner's premature or untimely death, but very few are aware of the fact that living too long can also be a risk from the financial point of view. Every person reaches an age, when he has to retire from active earning life. If he is an employee he retires with stoppage of income overnight or with sizeable reduction of income in the form of pension. A businessman has also to retire one day or the other.

The best way to provide for this inevitable loss of income stage is to purchase annuities sold by life insurance companies.

There are two varieties according to the time of vesting of annuity. In an immediate annuity, the purchaser of the annuity called annuitant pays a lump-sum amount as purchase price to secure regular annuity payment for him in future until his death. In Deferred Annuity the annuitant pays a single premium or agrees to pay premiums in future until he reaches the desired age, when he wants annuity to start. The premium/premiums paid accumulate with interest and the accumulated amount called 'pension corpus' provides him annuity at the desired age. Premiums under deferred annuity can be paid by yearly, half-yearly, quarterly or monthly mode. The Annuity-payment can be made in yearly, half-yearly, quarterly mode. There are various options available as regards duration of annuity instalment:

(1) Annuity for life. This stops on death.

(2) Annuity with guaranteed period of 5, 10, 15, 20 years and for life thereafter.

(3) Joint life and last survivor annuity to the annuitant and his/her spouse under which annuity payable on death of the purchaser will be 50% of that payable to the annuitant.

(4) Life annuity with return of a purchase price.

(5) Life annuity increasing at a simple rate of 3% per annum.

In case of Deferred Annuity the Annuitant can commute 25% of the pension corpus, calculated on acturial basis. Commuted value is tax-free. Pension will be calculated on remaining pension corpus. Pensions are provided by the employer to his employees. Annuity is granted by the insurance company. But both work on the same principle. Annuity income is taxable, as with other income. Pension is like salary as per provisions of IT Act. Hence, it is entitled to standard deduction u/s 16(i) of Income Tax Act. Premiums paid under annuity plans are eligible for tax-rebate u/s 88 of I.T. Act. However premiums paid for Jeevan Suraksha and similar annuity policies are entitled to deduction upto Rs. 10,000 u/s 80CCC, 80CCCB of I.T. Act. Annuity is paid in arrears, that is, at the end of the selected period. Annuity stops on death. Hence, the insurer requires existence certificate for continuation of annuity payments. No medical examination is necessary for purchasing an annuity policy, since no death risk is involved. Annuitants, it is said, exercise self selection.

Over a number of years, the Indian population has been ageing. As on 2003, prospective pensioners are 22.14 crores out of which 4.40 crores are covered by various pension schemes. Percentage of 60+ population.

11.30 crores (8.9%) by 2016

19.90 crores (13.3%) by 2026

31.40 crores (20%) by 2050.

There is thus great and immense scope for the pension market.

Group Insurance and Superannuation (Schemes)

'Group Insurance' is, in a way, an extension of *'individual insurance'* into *'Class Insurance'* which itself culminates in 'mass insurance.' In a single master policy, called *'master policy'* the employees/workers members of one group are insured for one year's Term Assurance (OYTA) renewable every year. The contract is between the insurer and the employer, though risk is covered on employees' lives. The group selection and group underwriting is followed. Size of the group (minimum 25), profession of the group, nature of the group, mortality experience of earlier few years, financial stability, growth potential — all these factors along with the composition of the group — age-wise — are also to be considered. The amount which employees will get will be decided by the employer — on the basis of age, salary, seniority, income etc. All the members are covered under the scheme, subject to eligibility criteria decided by the employer and the insurer. Usual criterion is 'actively at work' condition, which means that the employee should not be on leave on medical grounds when the group insurance policy commences. The premium under group policy changes every year because of participant-members' deaths, retirement, resignations, new entries. Even without these the premium would change, because every member would have became older each year and everybody's salary/wages would have gone up, entailing higher sums assured, which is normally fixed as one or two years salary. On the basis of average salary, a limit of insurance amount is fixed for every member, which is available without medical examination. *This is called free cover limit or no evidence limit. An individual who is found uninsurable under individual policy may be able to obtain group insurance upto free cover or no evidence limit.* If his eligibility, according to a predetermined formula, crosses this limit, underwriting will be done for this excess over the free cover limit only. At the end of the year at the time of renewal, a review of actual experience of death claims with assumed deaths is undertaken. If it is favourable, there is profit, which is calculated on acturial principles, the same is shared with the employer. This share is utilised to reduce next years' premium. If there is a loss, the same is also shared by the employer. This is called a profit-sharing system. Consequently the premium to be charged for the next year renewal would also change. This is called *experience rating.*

Group Savings Linked Insurance (GSLI)

Employees contribute the premium. A part is utilised to offer group insurance cover, the remaining portion accumulates with interest in a savings scheme.

Group Gratuity Schemes: Under the payment of Gratuity Act every employer is obliged to give gratuity to his workman who has completed more than 5 years of service, at the rate 1/2 month's salary for each completed year of service, salary consisting of Basic + DA, with a month consisting of 26 days. Under the Act, employer has to create a gratuity reserve fund for meeting future gratuity liability. This has to be certified by a qualified actuary. As an alternative, the employers can purchase a Group Gratuity Insurance Policy, when actuary's certificate is not necessary. The pre-requisite is that the employer has to create a Trust, which shall administer the Trust Fund. The scheme ensures that every member of the scheme is assured of 20 months salary in the form of accrued gratuity and group insurance covering future gratuity. Premiums paid are allowed as a business expense. At the time of introducing the scheme, accrued gratuity (Past service gratuity) can also be covered for which pure endowment one time premium is charged.

Group Leave Encashment Scheme (GLES)

Under an amendment to Companies Act made in 1988 and according to accounting standards, employers have to fund the liability in respect of leave encashment facility. The Group scheme provides for group insurance also upto Rs. 25,000.

Group Superannuation Schemes

The employers who want to provide pension to their employees without taking over the pension administration of the scheme can purchase this policy. Every month the employer transfers a fixed agreed amount, normally 1/2 month's salary-equivalent to the insurer. These amounts accumulate with interest and form the pension corpus at the time of retirement of the concerned employee, who has to inform the insurer about the type of pension he wants and the mode of payment of pension. Tax free commutation of part of the pension corpus can be made subject to I.T. Rules operating in this behalf. If such option is exercised, the pension amount would get reduced. It is usual under this scheme to utilise a portion of employer's contribution to provide Life Insurance upto the agreed limit. Pension contribution in that case will get reduced.

Mass Insurance schemes are mooted through Government initiatives. *Janashree Bima Yojana* provides protection to the urban and rural poor. 50% of the premium is subsidised from social security fund maintained by LIC and remaining 50% by members/nodal agency. Persons between 18 and 60 are covered for Rs. 20,000 etc. Death or permanent disability cover is Rs. 50,000.

Swarnajayanti Rojgar Yojana: Borrowers of IRDP scheme are covered for Rs. 5,000 for death and for Rs. 10,000 for accidental death. No premium is paid by the beneficiary members.

Krishi Shramik Samajik Suraksha Yojana provides lump-sum survival benefits and pension to agricultural workers. The member pays Rs. 365/- per annum, double the amount is contributed from the social security fund. Agricultural workers between the age of 18 and 50 are covered for Rs. 20,000 upto the age of 60. Premiums paid are also refunded with interest. If 10 years contribution has been paid, a pension of Rs. 100/- per month is paid to the member.

Shiksha Sahayog Yojana is an addition to Janashree Bima Yojana. This provides an educational allowance of Rs. 300 per quarter to students studying in classes 9 to 12, whose parents are living below poverty line and are members of Janashree Bima Yojana.

Important Legal Provisions

Life Insurance business in India is mainly governed by the Indian Insurance Act, 1938 as amended upto year 2000. The Act contains provisions regarding various aspects governing the life insurance business.

Definitions

Sec. (2(2) Policyholder includes a person to whom whole of the interest of the policyholder in the policy is assigned once and for all but does not include an assignee thereof whose interest in the policy is indefeasible or is for the time subject to other conditions.

Sec. 2(1A) Authority means Insurance Regulatory and Development Authority established under sub-section (1) of Section 3 of the IRDA Act, 1999.

Sec. 2(5B) Controller of Insurance means the officer appointed by the Central Government under Section 2B to exercise all the powers, discharge the functions and perform the duties of the Authority under this Act or the Life Insurance Corporation Act, 1956 or the General Insurance Business (Nationalizaton) Act, 1972 or the Insurance Regulatory and Development Authority Act, 1999.

Sec. 2(7A) Indian insurance business means any insurer being a company.

(a) which was formed and registered under the Indian Companies Act, 1956.

(b) in which the aggregate holdings of equity shares by a foreign company, either by itself or through its subsidiary companies or nominees do not exceed twenty six percent paid-up equity capital of such Indian Insurance company.

(c) whose sole purpose is to carry on life insurance business or general insurance business or reinsurance business.

Explanation: Foreign company means as expressed under clause (23A) of Section 2 of the Income Tax Act, 1961.

Sec 2(B)(1) If at any time, the Authority is superceded under sub-section (1) of Section 19 of the IRDA Act 1999, the Central Government may by notification in the *Official Gazette*, appoint a person to be the controller of insurance till such time the Authority is reconstituted.

Sec. 3 No person shall begin to carry on any class of insurance business in India unless he has obtained from the authority a certificate of registration' for the particular class of business.

Sec. 6 No Insurer shall be registered unless he has

(i) a paid-up equity capital of rupees one hundred crores in case of a person carrying on the business of life insurance or general insurance or

(ii) a paid-up equity capital of rupees two hundred crores in case of a person carrying on exclusively the business as a reinsurer.

Sec. 6AA(1) No promoter shall at any time hold more than twenty-six per cent or such other percentage of the paid-up equity capital in an Indian Insurance company. Provided an Indian company having share capital of more than 26% shall divest the excess after a period of ten years.

Sec. 7(a) Every Life Insurance company has to deposit and keep deposited with RBI office in India a sum equivalent to one per cent of his total gross premium written in India in any financial year not exceeding rupees ten crores.

(c) Every reinsurer, a sum of rupees twenty crores.

Sec. 13 Every Life Insurer in respect of life insurance business transacted by him *every year* cause an investigation to be made by an actuary into the financial condition of the life insurance business carried on by him, including a valuation of his liabilities. Authority has a right to ask for revaluation.

Sec. 14 Every Insurer in respect of all business transacted by him in India shall maintain a register or record of policies issued by it, showing name and address of the policyholder and the date of the policy and a record of transfer, assignment or nomination.

Sec. 27 Investment of assets equivalent to amount of liabilities on policies of life insurance as per IRDA guidelines in this behalf.

Sec. 32B Every insurer has to procure prescribed percentage business from rural areas, and

Sec 32C Minimum number of policies from rural/ unorganised sector/informal sector/economically and socially vulnerable classes.

Sec. 38 Deals with assignment of a life insurance policy. Assignment means transfer of right, title and interest to a third party, either for valuable consideration or out of natural love and affection. Assignment can be absolute or conditional. Assignment cancels nomination already made under Section 39 of the Act. Notice of assignment is necessary. Assignment can be made by endorsement on the policy or by a separate endorsement.

Sec. 39 ***Nomination*** is a right given to the holder of policy on his own life. Nominee is the person nominated by the policyholder under Section 39 of the Insurance Act, who can give a valid discharge for the claim amount, if the life assured dies before the term of the policy expires. If nominee is a minor, appointee may be appointed to receive policy moneys, in case of death of the life assured, during the minority of the nominee. Notice of nomination to the insurer is necessary. Assignment to the insurer for loan granted by it within the surrender value does not cancel the nomination.

Sec. 45 is known as Indisputability section. A life insurance policy cannot be called in question merely for a non-disclosure of material facts once 2 years period from date of F.P.R is over. The insurer has to prove that there was non-disclosure, it was on a material matter, life assured knew this at the time of making the proposal and non-disclosure was fraudulently made. These provisions do not apply to admission of age at any time and to adjust the terms of the policy, consequently.

Sec. 64V refers to the valuation of assets.

Sec. 64VA stipulates that every insurer must maintain solvency margin, (in accordance with Regulations framed by IRDA) which shall be at least fifty crores of rupees, (one hundred crores for a reinsurer.) It defines mathematical reserves net incurred claims and sum at risk. An insurer who does not maintain solvency margin shall be deemed to be insolvent.

Sec. 64(V)B stipulates that no insurer shall assume the risk unless premium is received in advance. An agent has no authority to collect premiums.

Sec. 112 permits declaration of interim bonus for policies becoming claim during intervaluation period.

Sec. 113 gives a valuable privilege to the policyholders, who have paid at least 3 consecutive years premiums. Such policies acquire guaranteed surrender value equal to 30% of the premiums paid excluding first year's premium and all extra premiums paid in this behalf.

Sec 113(2) states that a policy which has acquired surrender value shall acquire paid-up value on proportionate basis. i.e., number of premiums paid divided by number of premiums payable, into sum assured plus bonuses on full sum assured for the period for which policy was in force. This concession is not available to those policies which are covered by automatic premium advance scheme.

Sec. 114 gives powers to the Central Government to make regulations. Sec. 114A gives power to authority to make regulations. There are 30 items about which IRDA can frame regulations. Ombudsman rules were framed in 1998 by Central Government under Section 114(1) (then current) for the redressal of grievances of policyholders to protect their interest and to regulate, promote, and ensure orderly growth of the insurance industry. After the amendments in 1999, this power now vests with IRDA u/s sub-section (2c) of Sec. 114(1). The Ombudsman acts as an arbitrator in disputes relating to partial or total repudiation of claims, any dispute regarding premium paid or payable, any dispute regarding legal construction of the policy relating to claims, delay in settlement of claims, non-issue of any insurance document after receipt of premium.

Ombudsman has no judicial authority. Complainant and the insurer can make submissions but lawyers cannot appear. Complaint can be preferred if the insurer rejects the complaint or no reply is received within one month or the reply is not satisfactory. The complaint should not have been preferred to any court or any consumers forum or arbitration. Ombudsman has to make recommendations within one month. Insurer has to comply within 15 days. If the complainant does not accept the recommendation, Ombudsman shall pass an award within 3 months. Ombudsman's monetary limit is Rs. 20,00,000. If the complainant does not intimate the acceptance, award cannot be implemented. There are at present 12 Ombudsmen operating in the country, on a regional basis.

Consumer Protection Act, 1986

Consumer has four basic rights. The right to safety, the right to be informed, the right to choose and the right to be heard (redressal). Under COPA, consumer has a right to approach District Consumers Grievance Redressal Forum (CDRF), whose financial limit is Rs. 20,00,000/-. Consumer has to allege defect or deficiency in service. Insurance is a service. Hence, aggrieved policyholders can approach Consumer's Forum, which consists of a presiding officer, who is a legally qualified and experienced person and two other members of whom one shall be a woman member. Appeal lies to the State Commission, whose original jurisdiction is

Rs. 100,00,000. Appeal against State Commission's decision and complaints over Rs. 100,00,000 lie to the National Commission.

Life Insurance Corporation Act, 1956

LICI is a body corporate consisting of not more than 16 members, of whom one is appointed as chairman. Monopoly given to LIC to transact life insurance business in India provided by Sec. 30 of the Act, has come to an end by adding Sec. 30 A therein. LIC has to perform valuation of its assets and liabilities u/s 26 and place the report before the Loksabha. U/s 28 ninety five percent of the allocable surplus is to be distributed to the with profit holders by way of bonus. Government of India gets 5% of the allocable surplus, since Government of India has provided initial capital of Rs. 5 crores. In case of private insurers, not more than 10% of the allocable surplus can be allotted to shareholders. Section 37 provides that corporation's policies are guaranteed by Central Government.

Insurance Regulatory Authority Act, 1999: Sec. 3 of the Act establishes Authority which has superceded controller of insurance, who can now function under the circumstances described u/s 2B of the Insurance Act. 'Controller' shall be appointed if IRDA is superceded by Central Government u/s 19 of IRDA Act, 1999. IRDA consists of a chairperson, not more than five wholetime members and not more than four part-time members. Chairperson holds office not beyond 65 years of age and not more than a five years term. Members hold office for five years. Full time members hold office upto 62 years of age. Sec. 6 gives powers to Central Government to remove any member. IRDA has wide powers as contained in Section 14. Sec. 24 gives powers to Central Government to make certain Rules. Sec. 25 gives powers to IRDA to make Regulations. IRDA may establish Insurance Advisory Committee of not more than 25 members.

JUDICIAL PRONOUNCEMENTS

Life Insurance Company's business activities have been the subject matter of judicial review for a long time. A lot of case law has been built on some of the important sections –

more especially Sec. 38 (assignment), Sec. 39 (nomination) and (by far the highest) Sec. 45 (Indisputability). Prior to passing of COPA, the aggrieved claimant had to file a civil suit or file a writ petition, on selected issues. The cases now go before District Forums/State or National Commission, as the case may be.

(1) If the Life assured conceals anything that he knows to be material, it is fraud, and if he conceals anything that may influence the rate of premium, such concealment vitiates the policy.

Major Chopra vs. New Zealand Insurance Co. (Cal-HC 1967)[2]

(2) The proposer has a duty to disclose all relevant facts and information coming to his knowledge until the date of contract.

Ratan Lal vs. Metropolitan (Patna, 1959).[15]

(3) Since the policy is framed by the Insurer, the defect in construction has to be construed against the Insurer.

LIC vs. Shakuntala (1975 AP) Proposal as the basis.[16]
Anderson vs. Fitzgerald (1853) – Imposing clauses must be explained.[17]

(4) Principles of indemnity does not apply to life insurance (Dalby vs. India & London Life (1854).[18]

(5) If there is no insurable interest, contract is void u/s. 30 of Indian Contract Act.

(a) Alamai vs. Positive Government Security Life Insurance. (B'bay HC 1899).[19]

(b) Dr. Mani Shankar Pandey v. Allianz (Lahore, 1941)[20]

(c) Brahmadatt Shastri vs. LIC (All. 1966).[6]

(6) Warrantying the truth of the statements made in the proposal form by way of declaration is in order.

New India vs. TSR. Reddy (AP 1969).[3] All India General Insurance Co. Ltd. vs. S.P. Maheshwari. (Mad. 1960)[21]

(7) U/s 45 of Insurance Act, proof of material and deliberate fraud is necessary. Mere constructive fraud will not suffice.

LIC vs. Parvativardhini Amma (Mad. 1965).[7]

(8) The 'Date of Policy' does not mean date of commencement of the policy but date of commencement of Risk (F.P.R.)

(F.P.R.) Khamele vs. LIC (Bom. 1971)[8]

(9) For revival of policy also, 2 years' period is to be calculated from the date of the original policy.

Mithoolal Nayak vs. LIC (1962 SC)[14]

(10) Even if life assured dies within 2 years of the policy and the repudiation comes after 2 years from FPR Sec. 45 is applicable.

(a) Vaid Maheshwari Shastri vs. LIC (Cal. 1968).[9]

(b) LIC vs. Janaki Ammal (1968 Mad.)[22]

(11) Material fact is that which a prudent underwriter considers to be so.

Major BAS Chopra v. New Zealand Insurance (1967 Cal.)[2]

(12) Days of Grace should be calculated from the next day after due date.

T.G. Rajan vs. Asiatic Govt. Sec. Life (1939 Mad.)[13]

(13) Insurance policy covering suicide risk beyond one year is not opposed to public policy.

Southern Union vs. R. Jehan Begum (Oudh 1945)[23]

(14) Refund of premiums cannot be claimed under a void policy. Sec. 64/65 of Contract Act are not applicable.

E. Muthappa Chettiar vs. Venus Assc. (Mad. 1944)[24]

(15) Sec. 39 confers right to nominate with a view to ensure speedy settlement to claim, without prejudice to the question of title.

State vs. Narayan Dayama (1958 Bombay)[25]

(16) Nomination does not confer right on the nominee.

Shanti Devi vs. Ram Lal (1958 All)[26]

UNCONCLUDED CONTRACT

Insurer's acceptance is necessary to create contract.

(17) Proposal reached the office after L.A.'s death. There was no contract.

CERS vs. LIC (1993-NC)[27]

LIC vs. Mumtaj Begum (1993 NC)[28]

LIC vs. Bimala Routrai (1993 NC)[29]

(18) Rights of a nominee clarified. Nomination does not confer any beneficial interest. But insurer is entitled to settle claim in favour of the nominee who gives valid discharge.

Sarabathi Devi vs. Usha Devi (1984 SC.)[30]

(19) Nominee is a consumer within the meaning of COPA.

LIC of India vs. Chatur Bihari Lal (Appeal 29/89[31] Rajasthan SC).

(20) Principle of indemnity does not apply to life insurance.

Dalby vs. India & London Life (854 CB)[18]

TEST QUESTIONS

1. Describe the peculiarities of the Life Insurance Product.
2. What is a Term Assurance? What are the various forms of Term Assurance.
3. Whole Life Assurance is nothing but extended term assurance. Explain.
4. What do you understand by a combination plan? Give 2 examples of the same.
5. Which plan would you suggest for a person
   (a) with reducing income?
   (b) with floating income? Give reasons for your answer.
6. What is the basis for Keyman Insurance.

7. Write short notes on:
   (a) Children's Assurance.
   (b) Health oriented plans.
   (c) Guarantees and options.
8. Define rider. Describe various types of riders.
9. Annuities differ from Life Insurance Policy in significant respect. Explain this statement.
10. Explain special features of Group Insurance.
11. Describe special features of the following schemes:
    (a) Group Leave Encashment Scheme.
    (b) Group Gratuity Scheme.
12. Distinguish between Assignment and Nomination.
13. Explain the privileges granted by Sec. 113 of Insurance Act
14. Explain the working of an Ombudsman.
15. Discuss the Role of Controller of Insurance *vis-a-vis* IRDA.
16. Quote a few important court decisions on the subject of (a) Insurable Interest (b) Material Non-disclosure.
17. What is nomination? What are nominee's rights under a life insurance claim.
18. What do you understand by "unconcluded contract"?

❑❑❑

5

Life Insurance — Salesmanship

Objectives

To provide an understanding of the process of salesmanship so as to enable the prospective agent to imbibe the spirit and substance of the art of Life Insurance Selling.

Lesson Objectives

To enable the students to understand:

(1) Rules relating to agency.

(2) Qualities of a salesman.

(3) Code of conduct for canvassing business.

(4) Importance of giving after sales service.

Rules of Agency

An agent is one who acts for others. One who acts through another or by employing agents is principal. In the Insurance Industry agent is one who procures business on behalf of his principal — Insurer.

Sec. 182 of Contract Act defines Agent and Principal. *An agent is a person employed to do any act for another or to represent another in dealing with third parties.* The person for whom such act is done is the principal.

The Rule of agency is expressed in the *maxim Qui facit alium facit per se*. i.e. one who acts through another acts through himself. The principal authorises the agent to represent him. The relation created between the principal and the agent is a contract of agency. So the contracts entered into by the agent within his lawful authority have the same legal consequences as if the contracts had been entered into by the principal himself. Agent's relationship with the principal is different from the one of master and servant. Agent is not under direct control of principal, master has a right to direct the servant as to work to be done but also the manner in which it is to be done. Agent is bound to perform according to the directions given by the principal. U/s 183 of Indian Contract Act any person who is of the age of majority can appoint an agent. According to Sec. 184, any person can become an agent, but a minor agent cannot be held responsible to the principal. *No consideration is necessary for creating agency contract. An agent can act only to the extent of authority given to him.*

A life insurance agent in India is only a canvassing agent. He has no authority to collect premia or other amounts from the policyholder. If the agent has authority to collect the premium, the payment of the premium binds the insurers. It may be implied by circumstances (Halsbury). But if the remittances from the Agent are being accepted by the Insurer, there is an implied authority. However Sec. 64(v)(b)(4) of the Insurance Act states that where an Insurance Agent collects a premium on a policy of insurance on behalf of an insurer, he shall deposit with, or despatch by post, to the insurer the premium so collected in full without deduction of his commission, within twenty four hours of the collection, excluding bank and postal holidays. In Hindustan Ideal Insurance Co. Ltd. vs. B. Jayalakshmamma (1959 AP 562) it was held that if the agent collects the premium, remits them to the insurer who accepts the same, there is an implied authority in favour of the agent. However, the National Commission has held otherwise in LIC vs. CERS (194 CPR 106NC) that premium paid to agent is not payment made to the Insurer. In this case premium under a lapsed policy was paid to the agent, who paid the same the day after Life Assured's death. LIC accepted the premium, in the normal course of business, being ignorant of Life Assured's death. In this case, agent who got the bearer cheque displayed criminal negligence and committed temporary misappropriation. The National Commission observed that the claimants set up a false claim. It also observed that CPA 1986 cannot be misused for making unlawful gain or to harass public servants. LIC was awarded Rs. 5,000 by way of damages.

The Agent, has authority to do everything legally permissible for doing the act. If the agent does more than he is authorised to do and the authorized part he has done can be separated from the unauthorised part, the principal will be liable for authorised part. If both parts cannot be separated, Insurer will not be liable for the whole act. An agent has to act within the scope of authority conferred on him by the appointment letter, which itself provides that agent has no authority to collect the premium. Moreover, the appointment letter would be subject to the Insurance Act, IRDA Act, etc. Hence, the agent is bound by Insurance Act. Also LIC does not allow agents to collect premium, except first premium deposit, along with proposal form. If agent collects renewal premium on his own, it would be a violation of the terms of the appointment letter as well as legal provisions in this behalf. Agent's (Licensing) Regulations 2000 read with Sec. 42 of Insurance Act, prohibit collection of premium by the agent. Where agent fills the proposal form; though IRDA guidelines do not permit this, unless the proposer is illiterate, the Insurer shall not be bound by this act of agents, whose knowledge cannot be imputed to the Insurer. Agent who fills the proposal form; for the client becomes client's agent and ceases to be an agent of the Insurer. A proposer who merely affixes his signature to a proposal which contains an untrue statement, cannot proclaim his innocence by stating that he signed without reading the answers or that the agent knew that replies were inaccurate.

Section 2(10) of Insurance Act provides a definition. *"Insurance Agent means an agent licensed under Section 42 who receives or agrees to receive payment by way of commission or other remuneration in consideration of his soliciting or procuring insurance business including relating to the continuance, renewal or revival of policies of insurance.* Various kinds of insurance business have been described in the Insurance Act. Fire Insurance business (Sec. 6A) General Insurance business (2(6)B), Life insurance business (Sec. 2(11) Marine insurance business, (Sec. 2(13A) and Miscellaneous insurance business 2(13B).

Knowledge of Insurance Agent cannot be imputed to insurer. Insurer is not liable. Newsholme Brothers vs. Road Transport & General Insurance Co. Ltd. KB(1929)356.[32] Here the proposal form was filled by the Agent of the Insurance Company, who did not present history of previous accident. The motor bus was involved in an accident. The Company repudiated the liability. This was upheld by the highest court.

In a case where the agent while filling the proposal form did not mention that the earlier proposal had been accepted with an extra premium, repudiation action was upheld by the Calcutta High Court. It was ruled that the agent filling the proposal form for the proposer, ceases to be an Insurance agent. Even if the imputed knowledge had been disclosed to the agent by the proposer, agent's knowledge could not be imputed to the insurer. A.F. Ferguson & Co. vs. Lalit Mohan Ghosh (1954 Pat.)[33]

However, if the proposer is illiterate and cannot be blamed for non-disclosure, knowledge of the agent may be taken as the knowledge of the Insurer. If the language of the proposal form and the language of answers differ, it must be established that the statements in the proposal form had been explained to the proposer in his mother tongue and that he signed the proposal only after understanding their significance.

Different kinds of Intermediaries

An Agent can be general agent or a special agent. A General agent has the authority to act for his principal in all matters in a specified area. A special agent is one who has authority to do special acts or to represent the principal in particular act or transaction. General agent has no implied authority to do anything that is normally outside the scope of agency contract. Special agent has implied authority to do those acts which are incidental to or necessary for carrying out the contracted work or duties.

IRDA Act defines Intermediary or Insurance Intermediary to include insurance brokers, reinsurance brokers, insurance consultants, surveyors and loss assessors.

But IRDA (Insurance Advertisement) Regulations 2000, add to this list any other person representing or assisting an insurer in one or more of the following:

(i) Soliciting, negotiating, procuring or effectuating an insurance contract or a renewal of an insurance contract.

(ii) disseminating information relating to coverage or rates

(iii) forwarding an insurance application.

(iv) servicing and delivering an insurance policy or contract.

(v) inspecting a risk.

(vi) setting a rate.

(vii) investigating or assessing a claim or loss.

(viii) transacting a matter after effectuation of a contract or

(ix) representing or assisting an insurer or other person in any other manner in the transaction of insurance with respect to a subject of insurance resident, located or to be performed in India.

IRDA (Licensing of Insurance Agents) Resolution 2000

Sec. 2(e) defines *Corporate agent* as a person other than an individual as specified in clause (i).

Sec. 2(d) defines *insurance agent* as one who holds a licence to act as an insurance agent for a life insurer and/or a general insurer.

Sec. 2(i) Person means (i) an individual (ii) a firm or a company formed under Companies Act, 1956 and includes a banking company.

Insurance Act 1938 defines various agents as follows:

Sec. 2(5A) Chief agent means a person who not being a salaried employee of an insurer, in consideration of any commission.

(i) Performs any administrative and organising function for the insurer and

(ii) Procures life insurance business for the insurer by the employing or causing to be employed insurance agents on behalf of the insurer.

> Sec. 2(10) Insurance Agent means an insurance agent licensed under Section 42 who receives or agrees to receive payment by way of commission or other remuneration in consideration of his soliciting or procuring insurance business, including business relating to the continuance, renewal or revival of policies of insurance

Sec. 2(13) defines managing agents.

Sec. 2(17) special agent means a person who not being a salaried employee of an insurer in consideration of any commission, procures life insurance business for the insurer whether wholly or in part, by employing or causing to be employed insurance agents on behalf of the insurer, but does not include a chief agent.

IRDA (Licensing of corporate agents) Regulations 2002 give definitions of the following agents:

Reg. 2(e) *Composite corporate agent* means a corporate agent who holds a licence to act as an insurance agent for a life insurer and a general insurer. This is similar to individual composite insurance agent and defined in Sec. 2(d) of IRDA (Licensing of Insurance Agents) Regulations 2002.

2(f) *Corporate Agent* means any person specified in clause (k) and licensed to act as such.

2(g) *Corporate Insurance Executive* means a director or a partner or one or more of its officers or employees so designated by it and in the case of any other person the chief executive or one or more of its employees designated by him.

2(h) *Designated person* means an officer normally in charge of marketing operations and authorised by the Authority to issue or renew licences.

2(k) gives a very wide definition of 'Person': a firm, a company, a banking company, corresponding new bank, regional rural bank, a co-operative society including a cooperative bank, a panchayat or local authority, NGO, micro-lending finance organisation or a non-banking financial company.

2(n) *Specified person* means a director or a partner or one or more of its officers or other employees so designated by the corporate agent and in case of any other person, the Chief Executive or one or more of the employees designated by him, who is responsible for soliciting and procuring insurance business on behalf of the corporate agent.

A Corporate Agent receives commission. A specified person shall be an employee of the Corporate agent. *A Corporate agent gets a licence for a period of three years for which he pays a fee of Rs. 250. A specified person gets a certificate for a period of three years on payment of Rs. 500.* On ceasing to be an employee specified person's, certificate will have to be surrendered to the Corporate agent.

The procedure and qualifications to become eligible for being appointed as an agent are stipulated in Sec. 42 of the Insurance Act 1938.

The intending person must have passed Xth Std. examination from a recognised body, if he belongs to a rural area, otherwise he must have passed XII Std. He must be over 18 years. He must have undergone 100 hours practical training from recognised Institute (by IRDA) and should have passed the qualifying examination conducted by a recognised Institute (by IRDA). At present, the Insurance Institute of India is authorised to conduct an examination for individual agents. The Indian Institute of Bankers is authorised to conduct an examination for Bank Assurance and for Corporate (Bank) Agents and National Insurance Academy for Brokers. For specialised personnel like MBA/CA etc. 50 hours training is required. Insurer can transact only life or non-life business. However, an agent can represent one life and one general insurance company. Such an agent is called a composite agent, and has to undergo 150 hours practical training. A composite special category agent has to undergo 70 hours training. A licence once issued will be valid for a period of 3 years, unless terminated earlier by the insurer. The renewal fee of Rs. 250/- has to be paid at least 30 days earlier but not earlier than 90 days before expiry date. Fine of Rs. 100/- is payable if the licence is renewed within 30 days prior to the date of expiry. Once the date of expiry is over, IRDA may renew licence in appropriate cases, subject to a fine of Rs. 750.

Brokers

IRDA has created a new category of agents called Brokers in terms of IRDA (Brokers Insurance) Regulations 2002. *There are three kinds of brokers:*

(i) Direct Broker — to arrange for the placement of insurance of clients with insurers. He can be a composite broker also.

(ii) A Reinsurance broker is authorised to place reinsurance business of clients who are insurers with reinsurer.

(iii) A composite broker is authorised to handle both direct business and reinsurance business.

A broker gets a licence for a period of 3 years from IRDA. The licence fee is Rs. 25,000, Rs. 75,000 and Rs. 1,25,000 for Direct Broker, reinsurance broker and composite broker respectively. Renewal fees are 0.5% of remuneration received last year, but not less than the fees paid for the first licence. The maximum fees payable at renewal are Rs. 1,00,000, Rs. 3 lakhs and Rs. 5 lakhs for direct, reinsurance and composite broker respectively. A broker can be a firm a company, a co-operative society or any other person recognised by IRDA. The capital of the firm should be Rs. 50 lakhs, Rs. 200 lakhs and Rs. 250 lakhs for direct broker, composite broker and reinsurance broker, respectively. There should be no non-Indian capital. Every broker has to appoint a Principal officer, who should be a partner or director of the firm. Broker's employees should be graduates and have undergone 100 hours training and passed the examination conducted by National Insurance Academy. A Direct Broker cannot bring more than 50 per cent in the first year, 40 per cent in the second year and 30 per cent in the subsequent years from one client alone. Commission rates are slightly different from those payable to individual agents.

A Broker has to obtain a professional Indemnity policy — with limit of indemnity being 3 times the annual remuneration with a minimum of Rs. 50 lakhs, 250 lakhs and Rs. 500 lakhs for Direct Broker, for a reinsurance broker and for composite broker respectively. The uninsured excess shall not exceed 5 per cent of the capital.

Termination of Agency

A person is appointed as an agent by the insurance company, after he gets a licence from IRDA (which is issued by a Designated person, who is usually a marketing officer of the insurer). Licence is issued in terms of Section 42 of the Insurance Act, alongwith IRDA (Agents Licensing) Regulations 2000, provided the agent does not suffer from any disqualifications as ..tipulated in Sec. 42(4)(a) to (9). If the person suffers from any one of these disqualifications, designated person may cancel his licence, under Sec. 42(5) and also in terms of Reg. 9 of IRDA (Agent's Licensing Regulations 2000. Regulation 8(ii)(i) stipulates that no agent can apply for a fresh licence if a period of five years has not elapsed from the date of cancellation of licence by the designated person. The appointment letter will refer to the business performance expectations from the agent, as regards number of lives, number of policies, sum assured and premium income. Failure to perform business guarantee will also be sufficient cause for termination of agency. On cancellation of licence, designated person has to recover from him the licence and the identity card issued to him (Reg. 42(9) of IRDA Regulations.

Essential Qualities of an Insurance Agent

An Insurance Agent is defined under Sec. 2(10) of Insurance Act, 1938. He gets a licence under Sec. 42 of Insurance Act. His role and functions are described in his appointment letter. He is also subject to IRDA (Agents) Regulations 2000 which prescribe a code of conduct for him and state the do's and don'ts for him. Agents may be termed differently e.g., Advisor and/or Consultant. All the same his basic duties are the same everywhere. He has to solicit and procure insurance business, for which he is remunerated by way of commission, which is a fixed percentage of the premium.

> Section 40A of Insurance Act prescribes maximum caps on rates of commission as follows (as percentage of premium)
>
> | | | |
> |---|---|---|
> | A | Immediate annuity | 2% |
> | | Deferred Annuity with single premium or one premium | |
> | B. | Deferred Annuity other than single premium | |
> | | First year's premium | 7½ |
> | | Each Renewal Premium | 2% |
> | C. | Other cases | |
> | | First year | 35% |
> | | Second and third year | 7½% each |
> | | Fourth year onwards | 5% |
>
> A new insurer can pay during the first ten years of its operations, forty percent of the first year's premium as commission to the agent.

These attractive rates of commission are offered to the agent, because *he is performing an important task of selling an idea or promise relating to an intangible product.* It is not easy to sell an intangible product. Agents are sometimes called dream merchant as well. A Life Insurance agent sells a promise, which will be performed in future. The selling techniques therefore differ. Qualities required of a life insurance salesman are therefore substantially different from those required of salesmen of tangible products.

As a part of his activities, the Agent has to

(a) Contact prospects for life insurance

(b) Assess their needs and

(c) Effect a sale

(d) Complete all formalities relating to filling of proposal form and other related forms, collect the amount sufficient to cover first premium and ensure that the insurer gives his decision, which should be conveyed promptly to the proposer.

Prospect is the intending purchaser of the insurance product. Agent has to ensure that the prospect is convinced about the efficacy of purchasing life insurance, which would provide succour to the family in case of unfortunate premature death before completing the normal expected life span. When he agrees to do so, the agent has to get the proposal form duly filled in by him and signed by the proposer (prospect) alongwith cheque for the payment of amount of first premium. This stage in the selling process is called *close*.

Agent's duty does not end with the sale. He has to keep in touch with the policyholder to make sure that renewal premiums are paid in time, nominations are made or changed, and to assist in settlement of claims.

Life insurance is a service based industry, sales accompanied by service is the sure way of winning the confidence of policyholders. A satisfied policyholder himself recommends agent's name to his relatives, friends, acquaintances. Thus he becomes a centre of influence for the agent.

The agent has to imbibe a set of good qualities if he wants to present himself as an ideal salesman and become a role —model for others. The agent has therefore to pay attention to his personal development. This would enhance his capabilities to function as an agent. The business done by him and the commission earned by him would be no doubt a good measure. But more important is the reputation he enjoys in the market. If he has it, he will get more references from satisfied clients.

The agent must be conversant with the product he is going to sell. In the competitive market, he will have to be familiar with similar products of the competitor. He has to know the drawbacks and deficiencies of the product. The special conditions to which the product may be subject should be well-known to the agent.

No doubt the agent works for his commission. But that should not be the only motivational factor. He has to keep the client's interests at heart and not his personal gains. If he does this he will observe that his business is also increasing steadily. Thus, proper customer orientation is necessary for every agent.

As a businessman the agent must have his time-bound goals — as regards his business performance on four counts — lives, policies, sum assured and premium income. He is going to get money by way of commission. Yet he may like to rise up the power-ladder of the company. He should attend seminars, workshops, training sessions to enrich his knowledge and keep himself abreast of the changes that are taking place in different areas, encompassing the life insurance business.

A Life insurance agent has to manage himself. Good record-keeping is a must for a life insurance agent. His skill, knowledge, materials, money and minutes must be properly harnessed. He has to keep a record of his activities and to try to reduce the cost of every operation. IRDA Regulations for agents insist that the agent gives good and continuous service to the policyholder. Hence an agent has to keep a detailed records of policies sold by him — as regards policy number, plan-term, sum assured premium, nomination. He should keep a record of date of birth and other important events in the life of his policyholder. He has to remind the policyholder regarding the due date of each premium. He can as well send birthday greetings or marriage anniversary greetings. He should keep a track of important achievements of his policyholder.

An Agent has to identify his target market. He may select a segment of the market in which he would like to operate. Each segment has its distinct characteristics and specific needs. The approach to each segment would be different. Specialisation in a particular segment would give him a sort of expertise e.g., Income-tax related sales, Married Women's Property Act — segment, Non-resident Indians, students going abroad, military personnel. Target-market segmentation has to be done on the basis of geographical location, age, occupation, religion, social status, income business- nature, technology etc. The approach to each segment differs.

Trustworthiness is a virtue, on which the agent has to capitalise for making his agency successful. Getting customer-confidence is a real key to life insurance agents' success. When trustworthiness is obvious, customer-confidence follows naturally.

Life Insurance contracts are long term contracts. Hence the agent has to develop long-term relationships. Sensitivity to a client's feelings has to be acquired and retained. Putting the policyholder's interest first is the right approach an agent has to follow. This will result in improved business earning, expanding clientele, less lapsation and a good reputation in the market. The agent has therefore to follow a set of good ethical practices. No doubt IRDA has laid down a code of conduct as to what the agent shall do and what he shall not do. But a real agent has to follow this code on his own.

He has to place his client's interests at his heart. His sale has to be based on the customer's needs. It should not be a commission-oriented sale.

He has to keep in confidence the information he gets about his clients.

Time Management

Time is also one of the resources of production and it has to be managed accordingly. Planning, organising, controlling, delegating, reviewing, correcting — all these management processes apply to time management as well. An Agent has only 24 hours at his disposal. Therefore he has to learn to manage and save this limited resource. He has to economise on personal conveniences and comfort and find more time to devote to his clients — for making a first call, second call, close etc. He has to learn how to make better use of time. He has to allot time to each activity according to its importance and urgency. He must learn how to prioritise various jobs and assignments. He will have to keep a record of time spent on each job. He should learn how to avoid wasting time on unnecessary or unproductive work. A few steps can be taken in this direction. Avoid doing a job in a wrong manner. Because taking a corrective action takes more time. Don't start on incomplete or inadequate information. Keep things in orderly manner. Take decisions promptly. Avoid indecisiveness. Don't get obsessed with perfection.

Relationship Behaviour

A Life Insurance contract is a long term contract. *The agent has to give service with a smile to the policyholder —*

until the claim stage. Hence, relationship with the policyholder assumes great importance. Customer Relationship Management (CRM) has assumed prominence in the present days of consumerism.

The agent has to observe *courteous behaviour*, a genuine and purposeful behaviour; not a mere pretended and affected behaviour. A proper attitude has to be developed. He has to understand the customer. He need not sympathise, *but he has to empathise with the policyholder.*

Listening to the other person is an important attribute which one must develop. Listening makes the other person happy and comfortable. The 'sale' becomes easier when the prospect is in a relaxed mood.

Motivation

An agent has to function as an independent professional. He cannot expect someone to come along and help him. He himself has to develop the urge to do. *This is called motivation.* Motivation is goal-centred and goal-motivated. It need not be confined to monetary or financial satisfaction alone. Non-financial motivations such as acquisition of technical knowledge, the desire to be ranked as a top performer, to be known as a specialist in a particular area, to serve the community can be the cause of the non-financial motivation. *Motivation leads to a better performance.*

Communication

Communication means transmission of a message to others in an effective and acceptable manner. An Agent has to be well-versed in communication skills. *It is advisable to make a written presentation to the prospect.* This can serve as a basis for further clarifications. A written representation makes a personal interview easier.

Good communication should meet the following requirements, so as to make it acceptable. It must state all *important facts*. The passive objections should be replied to before hand.

The language of the communication should *be courteous*. It should not offend anyone. The interests of the recipient should be kept in view. It should be in *simple clear language*. Technical jargon should be avoided. It should be brief and to the point. It should touch the subject directly. Language should not be verbose or *complicated*. The data presented should be correct and authentic.

Persuasion

An Agent has to imbibe persuasive skill. Insurance is an idea. It is very difficult to sell an idea. Insurance is a promise to be performed in future. It is an intangible product. *The agent has therefore to use persuasive skills to effect the sale.* The prospect should be allowed to talk. He should not be interrupted. He should not ask complicated, close-ended questions. His objections should be welcomed.

Analytical Ability

An Agent must be adaptable in analysing the prospect's needs. He has to take along with him a checklist of points that must be discussed during the first meeting.

Behavioural Aspects

An Agent has to deal with the prospect as well as with the office staff. He will have to deal with other fellow agents also. *He should not interfere in the business of other agents. He should not critcise other agents or belittle them before the prospect. The Commission should not be shared with the client,* not because it is in contravention of Sec. 41 of Insurance Act, but also *because it is unprofessional and unethical.*

Rules to Canvass Business from Prospective

The appointment latter issued to the agent by his principal i.e., Insurer, stipulates the terms and conditions of his appointment. This would state among other things, business targets which have to be achieved during the agency year. The appointment letter would be subject to laws of the land more particularly Insurance Act, 1938, IRDA Act 2000 and various IRDA Regulations. The two IRDA Regulations which prescribe the rules for canvassing insurance business by Insurance Agents are (1) IRDA (Agent's licensing), Regulations, and (2) IRDA (Insurance Advertisements 2000) Regulations 2000.

(3) IRDA (Agent's Licensing) Regulations 2000 is a comprehensive set of regulations. It provides various definitions, lays down a set of rules prescribing minimum qualifications, practical training examination, fees payable etc. It stipulates a strict code of conduct for canvassing insurance business.

Corporate (Agents Regulations) 2002

These specify a code of conduct for corporate agents vide Sec. 9 of the regulations.

Code of Conduct

9. (1) Every Licensed Corporate Agent shall abide by the code of conduct specified below:

Every corporate agent shall:

(a) be responsible for all acts of omission and commission of its corporate insurance executive and every specified person;

(b) ensure that the corporate insurance executive and all specified persons are properly trained, skilled and knowledgeable in the insurance products they market:

(c) ensure that the corporate insurance executive and the specified person do not make to the prospect any misrepresentation on policy benefits and returns available under the policy;

(d) ensure that no prospect is forced to buy an insurance product;

(e) give adequate pre-sales and post-sales advice lo the insured in respect of the insurance product;

(f) extend all possible help and co-operation to an insured person in completion of all formalities and documentation in the event of a claim;

(g) give due publicity to the fact that the corporate agent does not underwrite the risk or act as an insurer;

(h) enter into service level agreements with the insurer in which the duties and responsibilities of both are defined.

(2) Every corporate agent or a corporate insurance executive or a specified person shall also follow the code of conduct specified below:

(i) Every corporate agent/corporate insurance executive/ specified person shall —

(a) identify himself and the insurance company of whom he is a representative;

(b) disclose his licence/certificate to the prospect on demand;

(c) disseminate the requisite information in respect of insurance products offered for sale by his insurer and take into account the needs of the prospect while recommending a specific insurance plan;

(d) disclose the scales of commission in respect of the insurance product offered for sale, if asked by the prospect;

(e) indicate the premium to be charged by the insurer for the insurance product offered for sale;

(f) explain to the prospect the nature of information required in the proposal form by the insurer, and also the importance of disclosure of material information in the purchase of an insurance contract;

(g) bring to the notice of the insurer any adverse habits or income inconsistency of the prospect, in the form of a report (called "Insurance Agents Confidential Report") along with every proposal submitted to the insurer, and any material fact that may adversely affect the underwriting decision of the insurer as regards acceptance of the proposal, by making all reasonable enquiries about the prospect;

(h) inform promptly the prospect about the acceptance or rejection of the proposal by the insurer;

(i) obtain the requisite documents at the time of filing the proposal form with the insurer; and other documents subsequently asked for by the insurer for completion of the proposal;

(j) render necessary assistance to the policyholders or claimants or beneficiaries in complying with the requirements for settlement of claims by the insurer;

(k) advise every individual policyholder to effect nomination or assignment or change of address or exercise of options, as the case may be, and offer necessary assistance in this behalf, wherever necessary.

(ii) No corporate agent/corporate insurance executive/ specified person shall —

(a) solicit or procure insurance business without holding a valid licence/certificate;

(b) induce the prospect to omit any material information in the proposal form;

(c) induce the prospect to submit wrong information in the proposal form or documents submitted to the insurer for acceptance of the proposal;

(d) behave in a discourteous manner with the prospect;

(e) interfere with any proposal introduced by any other specified person or any insurance intermediary;

(f) offer different rates, advantages, terms and conditions other than those offered by his insurer;

(g) demand or receive a share of proceeds from the beneficiary under an insurance contract;

(h) force a policyholder to terminate the existing policy and to effect a new proposal from him within three years from the date of such termination;

(i) no corporate agent shall have a portfolio of insurance business from one person or one organisation or one group of organisations under which the premium is in excess of fifty per cent of total premium procured in any year;

(j) apply for fresh licence to act as an insurance agent, if his licence was earlier cancelled by the designated person, and a period of five years has not elapsed from the date of such cancellation;

(k) become or remain a director of any insurance company.

(iii) Every corporate agent shall, with a view to conserve the insurance business already procured through him, make every attempt to ensure remittance of the premiums by the policyholder orally and in writing.

(iv) No director of a company or partner of a firm of the chief executive or a corporate insurance executive or a specified person shall hold similar position with another corporate agent of any other insurance company.

IRDA (Insurance Advertisements Regulation) 2000

(c) "Intermediary or insurance intermediary" includes insurance brokers, reinsurance brokers, insurance consultants, surveyors and loss assessors, or any other person representing or assisting an insurer in one or more of the following:

(i) soliciting, negotiating, procuring, or effectuating an insurance contract or a renewal of an insurance contract;

(ii) disseminating information relating to coverage or rates;

(iii) forwarding an insurance application;

(iv) servicing and delivering an insurance policy or contract;

(v) inspecting a risk;

(vi) setting a rate;

(vii) investigating or assessing a claim or loss;

(viii) transacting a matter after the effectuation of a contract; or

(ix) representing or assisting an insurer or other person in any other manner in the transaction of insurance with respect to a subject of insurance resident, located or to be performed in India.

(x) servicing a policy or contract.

(d) "unfair or misleading advertisement" will mean and include any advertisement;

(i) that fails to clearly identify the product as insurance;

(ii) makes claims beyond the ability of the policy to deliver or beyond the reasonable expectation of performance;

(iii) describes benefits that do not match the policy provisions;

uses words or phrases in a way which hides or minimizes the costs of the hazard insured against or the risks inherent in the policy; omits to disclose or discloses insufficiently, important-.exclusions, limitations and conditions of the contract;

gives information in a misleading way;

illustrates future benefits on assumptions which are not realistic, nor realisable in the light of the insurer's current performance;

where the benefits are not guaranteed, does not explicitly say so as prominently as the benefits are stated, or says so in a manner or form that could remain unnoticed;

implies a group of other relationship like sponsorship, affiliation or approval, that does not exist;

makes unfair or incomplete comparisons with products which are not comparable or disparages competitors.

Advertisements by Insurance Agents

6. Every advertisement by an insurance agent that affects an insurer must be approved by the Insurer in writing prior to its issue;

(2) It shall be the responsibility of the insurer while granting such approval to insure that all advertisements that pertain to the company or its products or performance comply with these Regulations and are not deceptive or misleading.

Explanation: An agent shall not be required to obtain written approval of the company prior to issue for:

(i) those advertisements developed by the insurer and provided to the agents; generic advertisements limited to information like the agent's name, logo, address, and phone number; and advertisements that consist only of simple and correct statements describing the availability of lines of insurance, references to experience, service and qualifications of agents; but making no reference to specific policies, benefits, costs or insurers.

Advertisements by Insurance Intermediaries

7. Only properly licensed intermediaries may advertise or solicit insurance through advertisements.

Advertising on the Internet

8. (1) Every insurer or intermediary's web site or portal shall—

(i) include disclosure statements which outline the site's specific policies *vis-a-vis* the privacy of personal information for the protection of both their own businesses and the consumers they serve.

(ii) display their registration/license numbers on their web sites.

(2) For the purposes of these regulations, except where otherwise specifically excluded or restricted, no form or policy otherwise permissible for use shall be deemed invalid or impermissible, if such form or policy accurately reflects the intentions of the parties in such form or policy as published electronically or transmitted electronically between parties.

Identity of Advertiser

9. Every advertisement for insurance shall –

(i) state clearly and unequivocally that insurance is the subject-matter of solicitation; and

(ii) state the full registered name of the insurer/intermediary/insurance agent.

Endorsements and other third-party Involvement

10 (i) A third party, group or association shall not: –

(i) distribute information about an insurance policy, intermediary or insurer on its letterhead.

(ii) allow an insurance intermediary or insurer to distribute information about an insurance policy, insurance or insurance company on its letterhead.

(iii) distribute information about an individual insurance policy, or about an intermediary or insurer in its envelopes, unless —

(a) the third party is providing only a distribution service for the insurance advertisement and is not itself soliciting the coverage, and

(b) the insurance information is a piece separate from any other information distributed by the third party and clearly indicates its origin.

(iv) recommend that its members purchase specific insurance products.

(v) imply that a person must become a member of its organization in order to purchase the policy.

(vi) imply that a purchaser of a policy by becoming a member of a limited group of persons shall receive special advantages from the insurer not provided for in the policy:

Provided that a third party, group or association may:—

(i) endorse an insurance company or insurance intermediary's product and provide truthful statements. quotes and testimonials endorsing the insurance products to the insurance company for use in company's advertisements, so long as the language does not convey directly or indirectly a recommendation that the members of the organisation purchase the products.

(ii) Provide an insurance company with information about its membership and collect compensation.

IRDA (Agents Licensing Regulations) 2000: These provide for a comprehensive code of conduct — a sort of do's and don'ts for the agent, which binds him to the servicing of the policy from proposal to claims stage.

Code of Conduct

8. (1) Every person holding a licence, shall adhere to the code of conduct specified below —

(i) Every insurance agent shall, —

(a) identify himself and the insurance company of which he is an insurance agent;

(b) disclose his licence to the prospect on demand;

(c) disseminate the requisite information in respect of insurance products offered for sale by his insurer and take into account the needs of the prospect while recommending a specific insurance plan;

(c) disclose the scales of commission in respect of the insurance products offered for sale, if asked by the prospect;

(e) indicate the premium to be charged by the insurer for the insurance product offered for sale;

(f) explain to the prospect the nature of information required in the proposal form by the insurer, and also the importance of disclosure of material information in the purchase of an insurance contract;

(g) bring to the notice of the insurer any adverse habits or income inconsistency of the prospect, in the form of a report (called "Insurance Agent's Confidential Report") along with every proposal submitted to the insurer, and any material fact that may adversely affect the underwriting decision of the insurer as regards acceptance of the proposal, by making all reasonable enquiries about the prospect;

(h) inform promptly the prospect about the acceptance or rejection of the proposal by the insurer;

(i) obtain the requisite documents at the time of filing the proposal form with the insurer, and other documents subsequently asked for by the insurer for completion of the proposal;

(j) render necessary assistance to the policyholders or claimants or beneficiaries in complying with the requirements for settlement of claims by the insurer;

(k) advise every individual policyholder to effect nomination or assignment or change of address or exercise of options, as the case may be, and offer necessary assistance in this behalf, wherever necessary;

(ii) No insurance agent shall, —

(a) solicit or procure insurance business without holding a valid licence;

(b) induce the prospect to omit any material information in the proposal form;

(c) induce the prospect to submit wrong information in the proposal form or documents submitted to the insurer for acceptance of the proposal;

(d) behave in a discourteous manner with the prospect;

(e) interfere with any proposal introduced by any other insurance agent;

(f) offer different rates, advantages, terms and conditions other than those offered by his insurer;

(g) demand or receive a share of proceeds from the beneficiary under an insurance contract;

(h) force a policyholder to terminate the existing policy and to effect a new proposal from him within three years from the date of such termination;

(i) have in case of a corporate agent, a portfolio of insurance business under which the premium is in excess of fifty per cent of total premium procured, in any year, from one person (who is not an individual) or one organisation or one group of organisations;

(j) apply for fresh licence to act as an insurance agent, if his licence was earlier cancelled by the designated person, and period of five years has not elapsed from the date of such cancellation;

(k) become or remain a director of any insurance company;

(iii) Every insurance agent shall, with a view to conserve the insurance business already procured through him, make every attempt to ensure remittance of the premiums by the policyholders within the stipulated time, by giving notice to the policyholder orally and in writing:

After-Sales Service

Life insurance agents provide financial security to their clients, through the medium of life insurance policies. Life insurance contracts are long term contracts. Hence, by its very nature, this entails continuous service over a long period of time ranging from 30/35 or more years. During this long period the financial needs of the policyholder and his family change as he progresses in his life cycle. Therefore, the agent's duty and responsibilities do not stop with the act of sale. He has to render prompt and efficient service to him. Service-after-sale is of prime importance. Therefore, the agent should equip himself with adequate knowledge about the various procedures and practices of the insurer in after-sale service.

The usual services that are expected to be rendered cover following aspects: Age admission, nomination, assignment, alteration, revival of lapsed policies, policy loans and settlement of claims.

It should be appreciated that after-sales service has its own rewards. It helps the agent to keep in touch with the persons insured by him and to get a further new business from his policyholder or his family members. This is called repeat-sales. A satisfied policyholder himself serves as a publicity medium for the agent. The agent should therefore thoroughly acquaint himself with the various procedures concerning servicing of the policies.

Age Admission

Mortality, as we know, is a function of age. i.e., it depends directly on age. Premium depends upon relevant mortality. Therefore premium depends upon age. The higher the age, higher the mortality, higher the mortality, higher the premium.

Age thus presents a peculiar hazard from the underwriting point of view. Hence, correct age must be stated in the proposal form. Normally, insurers insist on admission of age. However, if for some reason, age is not admitted at the time of the issue of the policy, the insurer has a right to insist on age proof at any time during the currency of the policy. The policy conditions, benefits can be altered if the correct age is found to be such as to entail change in plan-term-sum assured on account of rules of underwriting in this regard. The minimum requirement would be to ask for arrears of premium with interest. If the age proves lower, difference in premium is refunded without interest. If on the basis of the correct age, the life assured is found to be less than 18 years, a fresh proposal form will have to be obtained from a parent since the life assured will not be competent to contract.

The age proofs are of two types, depending upon the extent of reliability as to their correctness: *Standard age proofs and non-standard age proofs*. Underwriting practices are different for these types. While standard age proof would be acceptable without any special conditions or restrictions because of age, non-standard age proofs require imposition of extra premiums as also restrictions as regards plan, term, sum assured etc.

Standard Age Proofs

(i) Certified extract from municipal or other records made at the time of birth.

(ii) Certificate of Baptism or certified extract from the family Bible, if it contains age or date of birth.

(iii) School or college certificate or extract from the school or college records.

(iv) Certified extract from service register in the case of Govt./Semi-Govt Organisations, reputed commercial/ Industrial undertaking or institutions.

(v) Identity cards of Defence personnel.

(vi) Domicile certificate.

(vii) Passport.

Non-standard Age Proofs

(i) Horoscope — normally not acceptable.

(ii) Service record where age was not admitted on the basis of verification of date of birth.

(iii) Employees State Insurance (ESI) card.

(iv) Elder's Declaration

Self Declaration (Unstamped)

Self Declaration (Stamped paper)

(v) Certificate by village panchayat. If it is found to be authentic, it may be treated as standard-age proof.

Assignment

Assignment means transfer of right, title and interest in the policy to a third party. Assignment of life policy to a third party is governed by Sec. 38 of the Insurance Act. Assignment can be conditional or absolute. *Assignment is thus a method whereby the beneficial interests in the policy are transferred to a third party — with or without consideration.*

(i) Assignment can be done by an endorsement or by a separate deed.

(ii) A notice of assignment is necessary. This governs the priority of assignment.

(iii) Insurer has to register the assignment and acknowledge as such to concerned person. Assignor must be a major and competent to contract. Consideration is necessary — which may be valuable consideration or for natural love and affection. It must not be opposed to any law in force. Assignee should not be subject to any disqualification. Assignment once effected cannot be cancelled at the mere will of the assignor.

Assignment can be conditional. The condition should not depend on the mere will of the assignor. The usual condition would be that assignment will become inoperative if the assignee predeceases assignor or assignor survives the maturity date. Absolute assignments are normally for valuable consideration. A policy can be gifted as well. Assignment of a part of the policy proceeds is void. Mere deposit of policy document does not amount to assignment. If the assignee is a minor even natural guardian cannot deal with the policy. If the proposer and life assured are different, the L.A. cannot assign the policy. In case of Children's Deferred Assurance, assignment can be done only after the policy has vested in the child. If the assignment is done on the policy itself no stamp duty is payable. On death of the conditional assignee, interest reverts to the assignor. On death of the absolute assignee interest in the policy is transferred to the heirs of the assignee. Assignment automatically cancels nomination. Valid assignment once made can be cancelled only by reassignment in favour of the original assignor. Nomination already cancelled cannot be resurrected. A fresh nomination will have to be made.

Nomination

Under Section 39 of the Insurance Act a holder of a Life Insurance Policy on his own life can nominate a person to receive policy moneys, in case of his death, during the term of the policy. Nomination comes to an end on maturity. Nomination can be done at the time of taking out a policy, or subsequently, by endorsement on the back of the policy. If no blank space is available on the policy, nomination can be done on a separate piece of paper, which should be pasted on the policy document. If nominee is a minor, appointment of a person to receive policy moneys, if the life assured dies during the minority of the nominee, has to be done. Several nominees receive policy moneys jointly or to the survivors of them. As such no specific share of the nominees can be mentioned. Notice of nomination is necessary to be sent to the insurer. However no notice is necessary if it is executed on the proposal form itself. Nomination can be changed at the will of the life assured. A Will may provide for the cancellation of nomination. In such case, after the death of the life assured, notice of change of nomination will be required from the executors of the will. In case of a joint life policy, policy moneys are payable to the survivor on the first death. However nomination by way of endorsement of special wording can be made to provide for a situation where both persons die in a common calamity. A distinction between the nomination and assignment can serve as a useful guideline.

Nomination	*Assignment*
(i) It can be done by mentioning the nominee's name, age, relationship and address in the proposal form. After issue of the policy, by an endorsement on the policy. It cannot be done by a deed.	(i) It cannot be done before issue of the policy. After issue of the policy, by an endorsement on the policy, or by a deed, which must be stamped.
(ii) The holder of a policy on his own life. i.e., the life assured can alone make nomination.	(ii) The absolute owner of the policy (either proposer or the life assured or the absolute assignee) or the person having requisite authority from such owners can make assignment.
(iii) It is effected where Insurance Act, 1938 applies.	(iii) It can be executed anywhere in the world.
(iv) Assured retains full control and can deal with the policy without the consent of the nominee.	(iv) Assured loses control over the policy. Absolute assignee is the owner of the policy and can deal with it.
(v) Need not be supported by a consideration.	(v) Must be supported by a consideration.
(vi) May be witnessed.	(vi) Must be witnessed.
(vii) Notice is required to safeguard the Nominee's interest.	(vii) Notice is required to enable the assignee to acquire priority over earlier assignee.
(viii) Nominee has no right to sue under the policy.	(viii) Assignee has right to sue under the policy.
(ix) It can be cancelled by life assured during the currency of the policy by cancellation of nomination, by a change of nomination or by an assignment.	(ix) It cannot be cancelled by the assignor, except by reassignment.

Nomination	Assignment
(x) Where nominee is a minor appointment of an appointee by the life assured only is required.	(x) When assignee is a minor, guardian is to be appointed by the father of the assignee.
(xi) Appointment can be incorporated in the wording of the nomination.	(xi) Appointment cannot be incorporated in the wording of the assignment.
(xii) No vested interest in favour of nominee is created.	(xii) Vested interest is created in favour of assignee.
(xiii) Nominee's right is only to collect policy moneys on the death of the assured and when paid by the Corporation.	(xiii) On receipt of the notice the Corporation has to recognise the assignee as the person legally entitled to receive the policy moneys.
(xiv) If nominee dies, the nomination becomes ineffective.	(xiv) If a conditional assignee dies, the right under the policy reverts to the life assured, depending upon the terms of assignment. If an absolute assignee dies the right devolves upon his/her heirs.
(xv) If the nominee dies after the life assured and before settlement of the claim, the policy moneys would be payable to the heirs of the life assured.	(xv) If the assignee (absolute or conditional) dies after the life assured and before settlement, the policy moneys would be payable to the heirs of the assignee.
(xvi) Creditors of the life assured can attach the policy moneys.	(xvi) Creditors cannot attach the policy unless the assignment was made to defraud the creditors.

Nomination and assignment are matters of common importance. Agent is required to guide the proposer/policyholder appropriately. Hence, he must keep himself abreast of latest legal position and also his company's procedures and practice in this behalf.

Revival

When the premium is not paid within the days of grace, the policy lapses, but it may be revived during the lifetime of the assured and when the policy is in force. The grace period is 30 days for all modes of payment, except monthly, for which 15 days of grace period is allowed.

Ordinary Revival Scheme

All the arrears of unpaid premiums with interest alongwith evidence of good health are required.

Special Revival Scheme

If a policyholder is not in a position to pay all the arrears of premium with interest, this scheme is offered. The date of commencement of policy is shifted to a date prior to the date of revival for which premiums have been received, such period does not go beyond two years prior to original date of commencement. Plan and Term will remain the same, provided new premium ceasing age or new maturity age, does not go beyond the maximum prescribed and/or the plan. Revised premium will be calculated on new age as date of commencement. Under this scheme, arrears of premium become minimal. However, following conditions must be satisfied.

(i) The policy should not have acquired surrender value.

(ii) Application for revival should be made after 6 months but within 3 years from the date of lapse. The new date should not go beyond 2 years of the date of commencement.

(iii) Such revival should be made only once under the same policy.

Revival By Instalment

There are some policyholders who cannot pay the arrears under ordinary revival scheme in one instalment and are not entitled to the special revival scheme. The arrears of premium with interest can be paid by instalment spread over two years, to be paid alongwith normal premium instalments. However, arrears of premium should be for more than one year. Minimum 6 month's premium should be paid at the outset.

Loan cum Revival Scheme

Under this policy a loan is granted within the surrender value presuming that all the premiums have been received. The loan amount is utilised to cover arrears of premiums.

Survival Benefit-cum Revival Scheme

Revival of Money Back Policies can be done by taking into account the amount of survival benefit that would fall due subject to Revival.

Policy Loans

Insurers grant loans on policy within the surrender value available under the policy. These loans are normally granted upto 90% of the surrender value. Notional paid-up value is calculated on the basis of the premiums paid. Accrued bonuses for the period for which the policy was in force are added to the paid-up value, if the policy is with-profits policy. The surrender value factor depends upon the duration elapsed and the total term of the policy. The longer the term elapsed, higher is the surrender value factor. In policies which are in a paid up condition 85% of the surrender value is granted as loan. This loan need not be repaid, however loan interest should be paid regularly.

Certain classes of policies are not entitled to a loan, since no surrender value is available under the policy.

(1) Annuity policies.

(2) Children's Deferred Assurance during deferment period.

(3) Temporary Term Assurances with or without return of premiums.

(4) Money Back policies.

(5) Minor's policies during minority.

(6) Minor assignee.

(7) Policies effected under Sec. 6 of the Married Womens' Property Act, unless the trustees are authorised to raise the loan.

(8) Lost policies.

(9) If there is a prohibitory order or attachment.

(10) If the proposer is non-resident in India.

Paid-up Assurance

Under Section 113 of Insurance Act, 1938, if after at least 3 years' premiums are paid, subsequent premiums are not paid, the policy will not lapse but shall be converted into a paid-up assurance, which is a reduced sum assured calculated on proportionate basis.

$$\text{i.e., Paid-up value} = \frac{\text{No. of premiums paid}}{\text{No. of premiums payable}} \times \text{Sum assured}$$

The elapsed duration is calculated by deducting date of commencement of policy (DOC) from the date of First unpaid Premium (FUP). i.e., Date of FUP – DOC = Paid-up duration. FUP is obtained by adding mode of payment to the date of last premium paid. (DOLPP)

An example:

Sum assured 50,000

Mode of payment: Yearly

Plan-Term = Endowment with profits 20 years.

Date of commencement 14.9.1993

Date of last payment of premium 14.9.2002

Hence Date of FUP 14.9.2003

DOFUP 14.9.2003

– DOC – 14.9.1993

Duration elapsed 10 years

∴ Paid-up value = 10/20 × 50,000 = 25,000

The bonuses declared and accrued for 10 years period will have to be calculated on full sum assured. i.e., Rs. 50,000. If 10 year's bonus amounts to Rs. 750/- per thousand sum assured, the total amount of bonus that must be added to the paid-up value is 50,000/1,000 × 750 = 37,500.

The total paid-up value = Rs. 25,000 + Rs. 37,500

= Rs. 62,500

This amount would be available to the life on maturity or on death if earlier. Thus, Insurer's liability stands reduced.

Once the policy is paid-up, it losses all additional benefits attaching to the policy e.g.

(1) Double accident and disability benefits.

(2) Survival Benefits under Money back plans

(3) Guaranteed and loyalty additions

(4) Term Riders

(5) Critical Illness Riders.

A paid-up policy is free from further payment of premiums but is subject to loan interest and charges, if any, already raised on the policy. Since the premium payments have stopped, surrender value will stop growing. Therefore, if the insurer finds that the outstanding loan with outstanding interest exceeds the surrender value available under the policy, after adjusting the loan balance of surrender value, if any, will be refunded to the policyholder. This is called *Foreclosure which is a right available to a creditor for foreclosing the loan.*

Surrender

> U/s 113 of Insurance Act 1938, if at least three years' premiums have been paid, the policyholder can surrender the contract for guaranteed surrender value (GSV) which shall be equal to 30% of the premiums paid excluding First years' premium and all extra premiums paid under the policy.

However, insurers allow more liberal surrender value, which is a predetermined percentage of paid-up value. For this purpose, Surrender Value Factor Tables are prepared. SVF depends upon number of premiums paid and outstanding term of the policy. As premium paid term increases, SVF increases. However, it is always less than the percentage of premiums paid upto the date of paid-up. This happens for the following reasons.

The insurer deducts a certain *charge for the risk already covered.* In other words, there is recovery of premium for the risk already covered. Normally a policyholder who is not in good health will be inclined to keep his policy in force. The other side of this statement is that those who surrender the policy are, as a group, in good health. If such persons leave the insurance scheme, it represents *adverse selection* against the insurer. In order to discourage this, the insurer makes some deductions from the 'Policy Reserve' which is available under the policy. Lastly, the heavy initial expenses which the insurer has to incur to bring the policy into his books, such as agent's higher commissions, medical fees, policy preparation charges including Insurance stamps, heavy publicity and advertising expenditure, which are mainly for booking new business, cannot be recovered from the policy holder in one lump sum initially. Hence, it is spread over the entire policy duration. This amounts to amortisation of expenses. If the policy holder gets out of the scheme, the insurer is deprived of the recoveries planned from future premiums receivable. He has to recover this amount. Lastly, 'surrender' amounts to cancellation of contract. Hence, the party which is contracting out has to pay damages to the other party.

Surrender amounts to cancellation of contract. Policy has to be cancelled. Payment is to be made against the full and final discharge of insurer's liability under the contract. Surrender goes against the interests of the policyholder, since he loses valuable risk cover.

Some types of policies cannot be surrendered.

(i) If the assignee is minor.

(ii) If beneficiary under a MWPA Policy is minor.

(iii) If any HUF coparcener is minor.

(iv) If the policyholder or conditional assignee is insane or insolvent, of which notice is received.

(v) If policyholder or assignee is IT defaulter.

(vi) If court's prohibitory order is received.

(vii) Annuities.

(viii) Certain Term Assurances.

A policy which has been surrendered can be reinstated within six months of surrender, subject to evidence of good health and other requirements.

Lost Policy

Policy Document is an evidence of contract. Hence, if policy document is lost, contract is not lost. But insurer needs policy document for discharging some of the contractual liabilities. The policyholder himself needs it for security/loan etc. The loss or destruction of the policy does not absolve the insurer of his liability.

Ordinarily, insurer issues a duplicate policy. In case of matured policy, Indemnity bond may have to be furnished. For surrender also, original document may be necessary. The policyholder must give full particulars about the loss of the policy. An advertisement of the loss of policy will have to be inserted in a newspaper. Surety's declaration would be necessary. An Indemnity Bond with surety would be necessary if sum assured is large. If the policy is lost by theft, copy of FIR filed with the police would be necessary. When a policy is lost by fire, a report from fire authority may be necessary. Badly mutilated policy will have to be produced for inspection by the insurer.

Alteration in Policies

Since life insurance contracts are for a long term, the policyholder may feel a need to have terms of contract altered, provided the insurer, who is the other party to the contract agrees to effect such alterations. Certain policies will have in built alterations. No alterations are allowed as a rule within first year of the policy. If the alteration involves lower rate of premium, such alteration will not be allowed. *Any alteration involving adverse selection against the insurer will not be allowed.* However certain alterations have to be allowed even during the first year of the policy. e.g. correction in the policy, name, alteration in name, changes due to Exchange Control Regulations, bringing the policy under provisions of Married Women's Property Act, alterations due to change in age.

Certain alterations are not permissible:

(i) The premium rate gets lower.

(ii) Increase in term/premium paying period.

(iii) Increase in sum assured.

(iv) With-profit to without-profit.

(v) Reduction in sum assured below the minimum.

(vi) Paid-up/lapsed policy.

(vi) Periodical premium to single premium.

Alterations can also be classified as:

Compulsory: Such as change of name due to marriage, adoption, correction in policies change in currency.

Automatic: Increase in sum assured, premium if policy conditions provide for the same.

Decrease in premium: Due to automatic removal of extra premium.

Optional: Settlement Options.

Settlement of Claims

Claim is a demand for performance of the promise given by the insurer to the insured, who has performed his part of the promise i.e., *he has paid all the premiums.* Now he wants the insurer to settle the claim. An Agent has a role to play in this process. During the currency of the policy, the agent has to ensure that the policyholder pays premiums on time, his age stands admitted, there is nomination under the policy — so that settlement of the claim becomes easier. This is one of the most important sales services. If agent succeeds in giving satisfactory service on this count, he creates good will. He may get new business from the claimant, his family members, relatives and acquaintances.

Claims by maturity have been streamlined. With the help of a computer generated list, the insurer is in a position to settle majority of these claims before maturity date. The requirements are simple. Short claim form, policy document and discharge voucher, on receipt of which the insurer remits the cheque bearing maturity date. In a death claim, death intimation should come from the nearest relative or nominee or assignee. The requirements for death claim are original policy, claim form, death certificate and Hospital certificate, if the deceased had died in hospital. In case of early claims insurer needs investigation report, with a view to ascertain if there was any non-disclosure of material facts in the proposal form.

In case of accidental/natural death, FIR, Panchanama, Inquest Report, Post Mortem Report and Chemical Analyser's

Report if death occurred whilst under influence of liquor, narcotics or drugs or poison would be necessary. This results in delay of the settlement of claim. The Agent should be generally aware of these requirements. He should also be conversant with usual restrictive clauses such as suicide clause, pregnancy clause etc. In case of missing persons, Section 108 of Evidence Act applies. Claim lodged after 3 years from the day it becomes due is time barred. Agent should be aware of these provisions and guide the policyholder/claimant accordingly.

SELF STUDY QUESTIONS

1. Explain the *maxim qui facit alium facit per se*. Are there exceptions? Quote legal pronouncements in this behalf.
2. Explain the importance of Sec. 64 (v)(B) of Insurance Act 1938.
3. Knowledge of the agent is not the knowledge of the principal. Explain.
4. Describe various types of intermediatories as mentioned in Insurance Act, 1938 & IRDA Regulations 2000.
5. Distinguish between composite agent and composite broker.
6. Who is a corporate agent? Distinguish between specified person and designated person.
7. Describe various kinds of brokers.
8. What are the circumstances under which agency can be terminated?
9. Discuss a few qualities for becoming a successful agent.
10. What is time management? How does it help the agent?
11. Discuss the importance of motivation and communication in an Agent's career.
12. Distinguish between:
    (a) Nomination and Assignment
    (b) Standard and Non-standard age proof
    (c) Ordinary revival — Special revival
13. Why are alterations necessary in a life insurance contract?
14. What do you understand by aftersales service? What is its importance for the agent?
15. State the requirements for consideration of claim on account of accidental death.

❑❑❑

Annexures

ANNEXURE I

Glossary of Some Useful Terms

Term	*Description*
Absorbed Agent Existing Agent	An insurance agent licensed on, or before the date of notification of the Insurance Agents Regulations, 2000, under the provisions of Section 42 of the Insurance Act, 1938
Age Nearer Birthday	The age nearer birthday is obtained by substracting Date of Birth from the Date of Commencement of Policy.
Life Annuity	A specified capital sum is paid by a person in return for a promise from the insurer to make a series of payments as long as the person lives.
Article 41 of Indian Constitution	**Right to work, to education and to public assistance in certain cases.** The State shall, within the limits of its economic capacity and development, make effective provision for securing the right to work, to education and to public assistance in cases of unemployment, old age, sickness and disablement, and in other cases of undeserved want.
Assignment	A life insurance policy is a property and an assignment transfers the rights, title and interest of the assignor (policy holder) to the assignee u/s. 38 of Insurance Act.
Bond	A debt instrument issued by a company or government or its agencies, with a promise to pay regular interest and return the principal on a specified date.

Claim	A claim is a demand by the claimant for the promise made by the insurer while entering into the contract.
Composite Agent	An insurance agent who holds both life insurance agency license and general insurance agency license.
Consumer Education	Consumer education refers to informing the customer about quality, quantity etc. of products and services.
Consumerism	Consumerism refers to policies and activities designed to protect the interests and rights of consumers.
Consumer Protection Act, 1986	An Act to provide for better protection of the interests of consumers and for that purpose to make provision for the establishment of consumer councils and other authorities for the settlement of consumer's disputes and for matters connected therewith.
Contract	A contract may be defined as an agreement between two or more parties to do or to abstain from doing an act, which is intended to create a legally binding relationship.
Contribution	A term used in insurance when one insurance company claims a contribution from another in settling a claim. This frequently happens in general insurance, and may also happen in other policies where the insured is dealing with two separate companies for the same property. A person cannot obtain more than the value of the property by insuring twice: each company will pay a proportion of the claim.
Corporate Agent	Could be a company, firm, panchayat, registered society, or a co-operative society. Every director or person holding charge of the office of the Corporate Agent shall possess the valid license to act as an insurance agent or a composite insurance agent.

Critical Illness	An added coverage of paying out a lump-sum on diagnosis of a specified critical illness or dreaded disease.
Death Claim	Death Claim is due on the death of the life assured during the term of the policy.
Dreaded Disease	These are diseases like AIDS and Cancer which might make a person terminally ill. Some companies do not distinguish between a Critical Illness and Dreaded Disease.
Economically vulnerable or backward classes	Economically vulnerable or backward classes means persons who live below the poverty line.
Employees Deposit Linked Insurance	Employees Deposit Linked Insurance scheme is applicable to all organisations contributing employees provident fund in terms of EPF Act, 1952. An employee is covered under the insurance plan subject to his having a maximum of Rs. 35,000 as balance in his provident fund account.
First Premium Receipt	Risk can be assumed by issue of First Premium Receipt. It is unlawful to assume risk without the receipt of premium, u/s 64(V)B of Insurance Act 1938.
Foreclosure	Foreclosure means closure or writing off the policy before its actual maturity. Foreclosure action is taken when two or more half yearly instalments of loan interest are in arrears and a period of ten months has elapsed from the due date of the first unpaid half yearly interest.
Gratuity	Under the Payment of Gratuity Act, 1972, an employer is liable to pay employees 15 days salary for every completed year of service, on the employee's exit for any reason, after five years of continuous service.
Group Gratuity Scheme	A Life Insurance Company scheme which provides for higher payments specially in the event of an employee's death.

Group Insurance	Group Insurance is a scheme which provides insurance benefits to a number of people under a single policy.
Guarantees	Certain guaranteed additions are provided to the policy holders, under certain conditions which cannot be changed.
Health Insurance	Health insurance is insurance against sickness and medical treatment, normally granted by General Insurance companies.
Huebner's Human Life Value Theory	The economic value of a human life arises out of its relations to other lives. Whenever continuance of a life is financially valuable to others, either to family dependents, business associates, or educational and philanthropic situations, the necessity for life insurance is present.
Indemnity	Any act designed to compensate a policyholder for a loss suffered, by the payment of money, repair, replacement, or reinstatement. In every case the policyholder is entitled to be put back in the same financial position as he or she was immediately before the event insured against occurred. There must be no element of profit to the policyholder nor any element of loss. General insurance policies are indemnity contracts, but personal accident and life-assurance policies are not contracts of indemnity as it is impossible to calculate the value of a lost life or limb (as the value of a car or other property can be calculated) and to put the property in pre-loss position.
Insurable Interest	A fundamental principle of insurance. The legal right of the insurer arising out of the financial relationship recognised under the law, between the insured and the subject matter of insurance. An interest (financial or otherwise) in the subject matter of a contract of insurance, which provides the person insured with the right to enforce the contract. An insurable interest (e.g. ownership of goods insured) distinguishes a contract of insurance from a wager or bet.

Insurance Agent	An insurance agent is an agent licensed under Section 42 of the Insurance Act, 1938.
Insurance Broker	An individual or firm whose full-time occupation is the placement of insurance business with insurance companies. Their business is regulated by IRDA reservations. The broker receives brokerage expressed as a percentage of premiums from the insurer.
Insurance Consultant	They advise the insured like brokers but get paid by the insured instead of the insurer.
Insurance Regulatory and Development Authority Act, 1999	An Act to provide for the establishment of an Authority to protect the interests of holders of insurance policies, to regulate, promote and ensure orderly growth of the insurance industry and for matters connected therewith or incidental thereto and further to amend the Insurance Act, 1938, the Life Insurance Corporation Act, 1956 and the General Insurance Business (Nationalisation) Act, 1972.
Insurance Surveyors	With the issue of policies, occurrence of loss and the resultant claim, was felt the need for persons who could examine the claims and determine the amount to be paid to the insured as reimbursement towards the loss. Such persons in India are known as 'Insurance Surveyors'.
Law of Large Numbers	The number of times an event occurs indicates the actual probability of the event to happen if cases involved are large.
Loan Policy	A loan is the grant of a certain sum of money against a policy within the surrender value. Loans are generally granted upto 90% of the surrender value for in force policies and 85% of the surrender value for paid up policies.

Married Women's Property Act, 1874	Section 6 of the MWP Act provides that a policy of insurance effected by any married man on his own life and expressed on the face of it for the benefit of his wife and children shall be deemed to be a trust for the benefit of his wife and children and shall not be subject to the control of the life assured or his creditors or form part of his estate. A divorcee or a widower can also take this policy.
Material Fact	A material fact is a fact which would influence the decision of a prudent underwriter in deciding whether to accept a risk for insurance and on what terms.
Maturity Claim	Maturity claim is due to the insured on his survival of the term of the policy.
Moral Hazard	Tendency on the part of the proposers to get into insurance scheme usually by resorting to nondisclosure of material facts.
Morale	Morale is the extent of confidence and optimism in a person or group.
NAV	Net Asset Value is the actual value of a unit of a scheme on any given business day. NAV reflects the liquidation value of the fund's investments that day after accounting for all expenses.
Net or Pure Annual Premium	The amount of premium required taking into account the interest component along with mortality aspect.
Nomination	Nomination is a way to ensure easy payment of policy moneys in case of death claims u/s 39 of Insurance Act.
Obligations of Life Insurer towards Rural Sector	• Seven per cent in the first financial year; • Nine per cent in the second financial year; • Twelve per cent in the third financial year; • Fourteen per cent in the fourth financial year;

	• Sixteen per cent in the fifth year; of total policies written direct in that year.
Obligations of the Insurer towards Social Sector	• Five thousand lives in the first financial year; • Seven thousand five hundred lives in the second financial year; • Ten thousand lives in the third financial year; • Fifteen thousand lives in the fourth financial year; • Twenty thousand lives in the fifth year; If the period of operation is less than twelve months, proportionate percentage or number of lives, as the case may be, can be undertaken. In case of a general insurer, the obligations specified shall include insurance for crops.
Office Premium	The amount of premium required considering the provisions made for administrative expenses, unexpected contingencies and fluctuations along with for mortality and interest.
Ombudsman	A person appointed to investigate grievances against complaints of policy holders – under Ombudsman Rules 1998.
Premium	The consideration payable for a contract of insurance. It is also the price of the insurance product.
Proximate cause	The dominant and effective cause of an event or chain of events that brings about the event. The loss must be caused directly, or as a result of a chain of events initiated, by an insured periods. This applies to General insurance policies.
Endowment Policy	A regular savings policy. Provides life cover on death during the term. Offers Investment and Risk Protection – both.

Reinsurance Broker	In reinsurance, the buyer is the insurer who has business in excess of its retention and seller is the insurer which has spare capacity to take the business that is offered to it.
Revivals	Premia need to be paid as per the contract. Non payment of premium leads to a lapse of the policy (lapsation may occur due to sheer neglect to pay or due to financial difficulties). Insurers facilitate revival of the lapsed policies.
Riders	They are a special policy provision or a group of provisions that can be added to a policy to expand or limit the benefits otherwise payable.
Risk	Risk is a condition where there is a possibility of an adverse deviation from an expected outcome.
Risk Management	Risk management involves identifying risks, ascertaining the impact of the risk and controlling it so as to minimize the impact.
Risk Premium	The amount required to meet the risk of death for given age for a period of one year.
Rural Sector	Rural sector is defined as a place which as per latest census has — • a population of not more than five thousand; • a density of population of not more than four hundred per square kilometer; and • at least twenty five per cent of the male working population is engaged in agricultural operations.
Section 64 VB of Insurance Act, 1938	No risk to be assumed unless premium is received in advance. Advance payment of premium before acceptance of the risk.

Seven stages of Man	• Learner 0 - 21 • Earner 18 -26 • Partner 22 - 28 • Parent 22 - 36 • Provider 26 - 36 • Empty Nester 44 - 50 • Enjoyer 55 onwards
Seven (7) C's of Communication	From the point of view of an insurance agent following things need to be kept in mind: • Completeness: Complete information needs to be passed on to the client. • Courtesy: Both the language and tone needs to be pleasant. • Consideration: The profile of the client needs to be kept in mind. • Clarity: Simple language should be used. • Conciseness: Be to the point without the use of redundant expressions. • Concreteness: Not being ambiguous. • Correctness: In terms of data.
Social Sector	Social sector includes • Unorganised sector • Informal sector • Economically vulnerable or backward classes • Other categories of persons, both in rural and urban areas
Subrogation	The principle that, having paid a claim, an insurer has the right to take over any other methods the policyholder may have for obtaining compensation for the same event. Insurer places himself in the shoes of the insured.
Surrender	A surrender is a voluntary termination of a contract by a policyholder.
Survival Benefit	Survival Benefit claim is due to the insured on survival to the fixed period during the term of the insurance policy.

Tabular Premium	This appears in the published tables of the company.
Tax Rebates in Life Insurance	U/s 88 of the Income Tax Act, 1962 all premium payments are eligible for rebate upto 20% for general public subject to a sealing of Rs. 70,000. U/s 10(10D) all income from the life-insurance policies on maturity or death is fully exempted from tax.
Term Assurance	A Life insurance product which pays out a lumpsum on the death of the life assured if he/she dies during the term of the contract. Offers only risk protection.
Termination of Agency	The licence of any insurance agent including an absorbed agent may be terminated by the Authority, if such agent suffers, at any time during the currency of the license, from any of the said disqualification mentioned in sub-section (4) of Section 42 of the Act, as the case may be.
The Insurance Act, 1938	An Act to consolidate and amend the law relating to the business of Insurance. It provides for the registration of insurance companies, and the various rules and regulation they need to follow. It also vests IRDA with enormous power to ensure that the insurance sector is managed well.
Underwriting	Underwriting is the process of classifying applicants for insurance by identifying such characteristics as age, gender, health, occupation, and life-style or hobbies. People with similar characteristics are grouped together and are charged **premium** based on the group's level of **risk**.
Utmost Good Faith	A duty to disclose all material facts relating to the risk to be covered. A positive duty to disclose, accurately and fully, all facts material to the risk being proposed, whether requested or not.

ANNEXURE II

Index of Legal Cases

1. Laxmi Insurance Co. vs. Bibi Padmavathi (1961 Punj).
2. Major Chopra vs. New Zealand Insurance Co. (1967(Cal.)
3. New India vs. T.S.R.Reddy (1961-AP)
4. Joel vs. Law Union & Crown Insurance Co. (1908 KB)
5. Godfrey vs. Brittanic Assurance Co. (1963 SJ)
6. Brahma Dutta Sharma vs. LIC (1966 All)
7. LIC vs. Parvativardhini Amma (1965)
8. Khamele vs. LIC (1971 Bom.)
9. Mahesh Vaid Shastri vs. LIC (1968 Cal.)
10. LIC vs. Dharmvir Anand (SC 1968)
11. Sun Life of Canada vs. Jervis (1943 All)
12. Sun Life vs. Nilratan Mukerjee (1938 Cal.)
13. T.G. Rajan vs. Asiatic, (1939 Mad)
14. Mithoolal Nayak vs. LIC (SC 1962)
15. Ratan Lal vs. Metropolitan (Patna 1959)
16. LIC vs. Shakuntalabai (1975 AP)
17. Anderson vs. Fitzgerald (1853)
18. Dalby vs. India & London Life (1854)
19. Alamai vs. Positive Govt. Security Life Insurance (Bombay HC 1899)
20. Dr. Mani Shankar Pandey vs. Allianz (Lahore 1941)
21. All India General Insurance Co. vs. S.P. Maheshwari (Mad. 1969)
22. LIC vs. Janaki Ammal (1968 Mad.)
23. Southern Union vs. R. Jehan Begum (Oudh 1945)
24. E. Muttappa Chettiar vs. Venus Assurance (Mad. 1944)
25. State vs. Narayan Dayama (1958 Bom.)
26. Shanti Devi vs. Ramlal (1958 All.)
27. CERS vs. LIC (1993 NC)
28. LIC vs. Mumtaj Begam (1993 NC)
29. LIC vs. Bimala Raytrai (1993 NC)
30. Sarbati Devi vs. Usha Devi (1984 SC)
31. New Sholme Bros. vs. Road Transport & General Insurance Company. (KB 1929-356)
32. A.F. Ferguson & Co. vs. Lalit Mohan Ghosh (1954, Pat.)

ANNEXURE III

PRESENT VALUE INTEREST FACTOR

$PVIF\ (i,\ n)\ =\ (1\ +\ i)^{-s}$

Period	1%	2%	3%	4%	5%	6%	7%	8%	9%	10%	12%	14%	15%	16%	18%	20%	24%	28%	32%	36%
1	.990	.980	.971	.962	.952	.943	.935	.926	.917	.909	.893	.877	.870	.862	.848	.833	.807	.781	.758	.735
2	.980	.961	.943	.925	.907	.890	.873	.857	.842	.826	.797	.770	.756	.743	.719	.694	.650	.610	.574	.541
3	.971	.942	.915	.890	.864	.840	.816	.794	.772	.751	.712	.675	.658	.641	.609	.579	.525	.479	.435	.380
4	.961	.924	.889	.855	.823	.792	.763	.735	.708	.683	.636	.592	.572	.552	.516	.482	.423	.373	.329	.292
5	.952	.906	.863	.822	.784	.747	.713	.681	.650	.621	.567	.519	.497	.476	.437	.402	.341	.291	.250	.215
6	.942	.888	.838	.790	.746	.705	.666	.630	.596	.565	.507	.456	.432	.410	.370	.335	.275	.227	.189	.158
7	.933	.871	.813	.760	.711	.665	.623	.584	.548	.513	.452	.400	.376	.354	.314	.279	.222	.178	.143	.116
8	.924	.854	.789	.731	.677	.627	.582	.540	.502	.467	.404	.351	.327	.305	.266	.233	.179	.139	.109	.085
9	.914	.837	.766	.703	.645	.592	.544	.500	.460	.424	.361	.308	.284	.263	.226	.194	.144	.108	.082	.063
10	.905	.820	.744	.676	.614	.558	.508	.463	.422	.386	.322	.270	.247	.227	.191	.162	.116	.085	.062	.046
11	.896	.804	.722	.650	.585	.527	.475	.429	.388	.351	.288	.237	.215	.195	.162	.135	.094	.066	.047	.034
12	.888	.789	.701	.625	.557	.497	.444	.397	.356	.319	.257	.208	.187	.169	.137	.112	.076	.052	.036	.025
13	.879	.773	.681	.601	.530	.469	.415	.368	.326	.290	.229	.182	.163	.145	.116	.094	.061	.040	.027	.018
14	.870	.758	.661	.578	.505	.442	.388	.341	.299	.263	.205	.160	.141	.125	.099	.078	.049	.032	.021	.014
15	.861	.743	.642	.555	.481	.417	.362	.315	.275	.240	.183	.140	.123	.108	.034	.065	.040	.025	.016	.010
16	.853	.728	.623	.534	.459	.394	.339	.292	.252	.218	.163	.123	.107	.093	.071	.054	.032	.019	.012	.007
17	.844	.714	.605	.513	.436	.371	.317	.270	.231	.198	.146	.108	.093	.080	.060	.045	.026	.015	.009	.005
18	.836	.700	.587	.494	.416	.350	.296	.250	.212	.180	.130	.095	.081	.069	.051	.038	.021	.012	.007	.004
19	.828	.686	.570	.475	.396	.331	.277	.232	.195	.164	.116	.083	.070	.060	.043	.031	.017	.009	.005	.003
20	.820	.673	.554	.456	.377	.312	.258	.215	.178	.149	.104	.073	.061	.051	.037	.026	.014	.007	.004	.002
25	.780	.610	.478	.375	.295	.233	.184	.146	.116	.092	.059	.038	.030	.025	.016	.011	.005	.002	.001	.001
30	.742	.552	.412	.308	.231	.174	.131	.099	.075	.057	.033	.020	.015	.012	.007	.004	.002	.001	*	*
40	.672	.453	.307	.208	.142	.097	.067	.046	.032	.022	.011	.005	.004	.003	.001	.001	*	*	*	*
50	.608	.372	.228	.141	.087	.054	.034	.021	.013	.009	.004	.001	.001	.001	*	*	*	*	*	*
60	.550	.305	.170	.095	.054	.030	.017	.010	.006	.003	.001	*	*	*						

* The factor is zero to three decimal places.

Annexure IV

PRESENT VALUE INTEREST FACTOR FOR AN ANNUITY

$$PVIFA\ (i,\ n) = \frac{1 - \frac{1}{(1+i)^x}}{i}$$

ali	1%	2%	3%	4%	5%	6%	7%	8%	9%	10%	12%	14%	15%	18%	20%	24%	28%	32%
1	0.990	0.980	0.971	0.962	0.952	0.943	0.935	0.926	0.917	0.909	0.893	0.877	0.870	0.848	0.833	0.807	0.781	0.758
2	1.970	1.942	1.944	1.886	1.859	1.833	1.808	1.783	1.759	1.736	1.690	1.647	1.626	1.566	1.528	1.457	1.392	1.332
3	2.941	2.884	2.829	2.775	2.723	2.673	2.624	2.577	2.531	2.487	2.402	2.322	2.283	2.174	2.107	1.981	1.668	1.766
4	3.902	3.808	3.717	3.630	3.546	3.465	3.387	3.312	3.240	3.170	3.037	2.914	2.855	2.690	2.589	2.404	2.241	2.096
5	4.853	4.714	4.580	4.452	4.330	4.212	4.100	3.993	3.890	3.791	3.605	3.433	3.352	3.127	2.991	2.745	2.532	2.345
6	5.796	5.601	5.417	5.242	5.076	4.917	4.767	4.623	4.486	4.355	4.111	3.889	3.785	3.498	3.326	3.021	2.759	2.534
7	6.728	6.472	6.230	6.002	5.786	5.582	5.398	5.206	5.033	4.868	4.564	4.288	4.160	3.812	3.605	3.242	2.937	2.678
8	7.652	7.326	7.020	6.733	6.463	6.210	5.971	5.747	5.535	5.335	4.968	4.639	4.487	4.078	3.837	3.421	3.076	2.786
9	8.566	8.162	7.786	7.435	7.108	6.802	6.515	6.247	5.995	5.759	5.328	4.946	4.772	4.303	3.031	3.566	3.184	2.868
10	9.471	8.983	8.530	8.111	7.722	7.360	7.024	6.710	6.418	6.145	5.650	5.216	5.019	4.494	4.193	3.682	3.269	2.930
11	10.368	9.787	9.253	8.761	8.306	7.887	7.499	7.109	6.805	6.495	5.938	5.453	5.234	4.656	4.327	3.776	3.335	2.978
12	11.255	10.573	9.954	9.385	8.863	8.384	7.943	7.536	7.161	6.814	6.194	5.660	5.421	4.793	4.439	3.851	3.387	3.013
13	12.134	11.348	10.635	9.986	9.394	8.853	8.358	7.904	7.487	7.103	6.424	5.842	5.583	4.910	4.533	3.912	3.427	3.040
14	13.004	12.106	11.296	10.563	9.899	9.295	8.745	8.244	7.786	7.367	6.628	6.002	5.725	5.008	4.611	3.962	3.459	3.061
15	13.865	12.849	11.938	11.118	10.380	9.712	9.108	8.560	8.061	7.606	6.811	6.142	5.847	5.092	4.676	4.001	3.483	3.076
16	14.718	13.578	12.561	11.652	10.838	10.106	9.447	8.851	8.313	7.824	6.974	6.265	5.954	5.162	4.730	4.033	3.503	3.088
17	15.562	14.292	13.166	12.166	11.274	10.477	9.763	9.122	8.544	8.022	7.120	6.373	6.047	5.222	4.775	4.059	3.518	3.097
18	16.398	14.992	13.754	12.659	11.690	10.828	10.059	9.372	8.756	8.201	7.250	6.467	6.128	5.273	4.812	4.080	3.529	3.104
19	17.226	15.679	14.324	13.134	12.085	11.158	10.336	9.604	8.950	8.365	7.366	6.550	6.198	5.316	4.844	4.097	3.539	3.109
20	13.046	16.351	14.878	13.590	12.462	11.470	10.594	9.818	9.129	8.514	7.469	6.623	6.259	5.353	4.870	4.110	3.546	3.113
25	22.023	19.524	17.413	15.622	14.094	12.783	11.654	10.675	9.823	9.077	7.843	6.873	6.464	5.467	4.948	4.147	3.564	3.122
30	25.808	22.397	19.600	17.292	15.373	13.765	12.409	11.258	10.274	9.427	8.055	7.003	6.566	5.517	4.979	4.160	3.569	3.124
40	32.835	27.356	23.115	19.793	17.159	15.046	13.332	11.925	10.757	9.779	8.244	7.105	6.642	5.548	4.997	4.166	3.571	3.125
50	39.196	31.424	25.730	21.482	18.256	15.762	13.801	12.234	10.962	9.915	8.305	7.133	6.661	5.553	5.000	4.167	3.571	3.125
60	44.955	34.761	27.676	22.624	18.929	16.161	14.039	12.377	11.048	9.967	8.324	7.140	6.665	5.555	4.000	4.167	3.571	3.125